Seddon The S

A celebration of 50 years of Seddon (Stoke) Ltd.

Contents

3   Introduction by Stuart Seddon

4   Foreword by John Seddon

PART ONE – The Story in Time

7   Chapter 1 Early Days
The Build Up from 1897 to 1939

19   Chapter 2 Building A City
The Second World War and its Aftermath

31   Chapter 3 - The Start of a New Era
Enterprise and Enthusiasm in the 1950s and 1960s

59   Chapter 4 - Strikes and Shortages
Seddon in the 1970s and 1980s

77   Chapter 5 - A Turbulent Time
Famine and Feast - the 1990s into the New Millennium

In 2005, Seddon's Derby office donated hundreds of daffodils as part of environmental improvements in the city. Adam Williams, Divisional Director, is pictured with a representative from the Groundwork charity

Contents (continued)

PART TWO – Company Culture

109 Chapter 6 - A Family Focus
The Seddon Family and the Seddon Companies

127 Chapter 7 – Parties, Humour and Sense of Community
Company Life in Stoke-on-Trent and Further Afield

147 Chapter 8 – On A Learning Curve
Apprentices and the Training Ethos

165 Chapter 9 - A National Reach
The Role of Seddon (Stoke) Across the UK

181 Timeline – Key Events in Seddon's History

187 Author's Notes

191 Acknowledgements

193 Index

Architect, Chris Taylor, of Christopher Taylor Design, pictured with Keith Harris of Seddon, on site at Albion Mill in Leek, Staffordshire.

2006 Painting Apprentice of the Year, James Phillips.

Introduction

Stuart Seddon
Chairman of Seddon (Stoke) Limited

This book has been written to celebrate the registration of Seddon (Stoke) Limited in 1957 – but a book outlining 50 years of our history would only be half the story.

'Seddon, The Story So Far' looks not just at the last five decades – but right back to the very start of the company in the late 1800s.

It was in 1897 when my Great Grandfather, John Seddon and his elder brother George started the family business in Bolton.

I cannot imagine how those two men – who both worked as bricklayers in the Lancashire mines – would feel if they could see how the company has grown to what it is today, a national organisation undertaking multi-million pound contracts across the UK – and now run by the fourth generation of the Seddon family.

Despite the growth and successes we have enjoyed, I feel sure George and John would be proud – and reassured - by the fact the business is still based on the firm foundations they carved out more than a century ago, namely to offer a quality service, to rise positively to opportunities and challenges – and to deliver a family-focused approach to business in co-operation with the wider community.

It is an honour to write this introduction to a book about a company that takes a pride in its future - and is proud of its past. For many decades, a sense of community, a commitment to training and a pride in our business have been the hallmarks of our company - and long may they continue.

I hope you will enjoy reading this book as much as we have enjoyed putting it together.

Researching the content has provided a wonderful opportunity for many friends to come together – sometimes after years of retirement – to reminisce about their time with Seddon. Countless memories have been brought flooding back that may otherwise have been forgotten.

It must be said that throughout the book we have mentioned many projects and people involved with the company. However, it would be impossible to mention all that have featured in our progress over the years and I apologise in advance for that.

To conclude, I'd like to take this opportunity to thank all those people who have played a part in the company's past – and those with a role to play in its future.

Stuart Seddon
March 2007

Foreword

John Seddon

I am delighted to have been asked to contribute to a foreword to this book – my greatest wish would be for another member of the Seddon family to be asked to do likewise in another 50 years.

Yes we go back a long way. It is 110 years since my Grandfather John, and his brother George, set up in business and 50 years since the Stoke Branch of G & J Seddon Ltd became a separate Limited Company. It is 55 years since I started working for the family business.

I remember my Grandfather very well. The most abiding memory is sitting on his knee when I was about 5 years old and playing with his gold hunter watch and chain which I inherited on his death.

He was a highly principled and yet very modest and quiet man – everyone seemed to love and admire him – a great

example to follow. I remember his opening the New Offices, Coronation Buildings, in 1953, and his Chairman's remarks at the AGM on the same day. He said words to the effect that "we should all be very proud as he was to be contributing so much in Company Taxation towards the wellbeing of our country".

It never crossed my mind to consider any other career prospects, so I left school as soon as I decently could – starting work as an apprentice bricklayer as my Father and Grandfather had.

1957 was the year in my life of major events. First Claire and I married and set up home in Newcastle, Staffs and second G & J Seddon Stoke Branch Office became Seddon (Stoke) Limited.

I really found my place at Seddon (Stoke) and worked hard and happily there for most of my working life. My Father, Ernest Seddon, was Chairman and Managing Director – I was appointed a Director in 1960 joining my two Uncles Frank and Jonas, Jack Finney and Jack Hulme who were on the Board - followed very shortly by Cyril Adams in 1963, aged 30 and Terry Smith in 1972 aged 32. We were a very young and successful team (the average age in 1970 was 35).

Looking back, we all worked really hard. The industry went through some very difficult times but we survived and succeeded when many competitors failed. We invested all our profits in the business and our people, our principal guiding policy was "to always keep your best people gainfully employed" which we have nearly always managed to achieve, even when there were major redundancies and unemployment in our Industry.

We have come a long way in the last 50 years – and this is only the story so far. I have enjoyed every minute of my work and could only have done so because of the full support of my wife Claire, my family, and all my many work colleagues over the years.

John Seddon
March 2007

Seddon The Story So Far

A celebration of 50 years of Seddon (Stoke) Ltd.

PART ONE

The Story in Time

George Seddon

John Seddon

Chapter 1 The Early Days

The Build Up From 1897 To 1939

For George and John Seddon **(pictured opposite)**, elevation from humble beginnings to success was little short of spectacular. Orphaned at an early age, the two brothers – of whom George was five years older – soon became self-sufficient.

Economic hardships and a lack of opportunities forced George to take his first ride down into the Lancashire pits to start his working career – at the tender age of 10. John followed his brother some years later and both lads served as bricklaying apprentices – building arches and supports underground.

The deep, dank atmosphere fuelled a desire within both youngsters for a better life, away from the darkness. In a characteristic display of guts and determination, George took the brave step of walking away from the mining industry, when he was about 18 years' old.

Viewing the skills he had acquired in construction as a passport to escape, the young George embarked on a journey to freedom from the mines - and took his younger brother out of the pit with him.

Historical details are scarce regarding what the two brothers did next and it is not until 1897, when George and John were 27 and 22 respectively, that better records exist of their business activities.

In Business

Company records show that in 1897, George and John started a small building company in Little Hulton, a village approximately four miles south of Bolton, in Lancashire.

The business, in those early days, was situated in a yard at the rear of the Horseshoe Public House. The pub was run by a lady who George and John called "Aunty Mary." She was not a blood relative, but someone who was supportive of the brothers' business and played an important part in their lives.

From the pub yard, the brothers ran their business enterprise, using a hand cart to travel to sites fixing roof slates and pointing chimneys in and around Little Hulton.

Business grew and a field was purchased, close to the Horseshoe pub, on Manchester Road, to house the expansion. As the business moved away from the handcart to horsepower, outbuildings were built. A measure of the growing success of the company was the creation of stables for the Seddon horses.

Opportunities did not fall at their feet but this life was a world away from the restrictions of the pits. The brothers' quality work and a determination to succeed were the reasons for their degree of success.

However, freedoms were to be short-lived at this point in history.

Britain was preparing to enter the theatre of war and life was to take a different step as the brothers' company switched operations to support the fight.

The Seddon Yard in the Days of the Horse
This picture shows some of the Seddon horses outside George Seddon's home. Despite the often-assumed unpredictability of horses, the then modern motor vehicle could prove far more dangerous. As the proud owner of a Model T Ford, George Seddon would start his journey from the site at Manchester Road with a push downhill from his men to start the engine. Unfortunately, on one occasion things did not go to plan and the car and driver ended up embedded in the front of the ornate building on the right of this photograph. Fortunately the building, had been erected by G & J Seddon and the company was able quickly to action repairs.

The Outbreak Of War

Prior to and during the First World War, George and John's skills in brickwork were called upon for the important task of building acid-resistant tanks for the munitions industry.

During this time, a lot of work was done in Yorkshire for a company, which used chemicals in the manufacture of bullets. The constant, all-pressing need to provide ammunition to front line troops meant that the Seddon brothers were to stay on English soil throughout the war, undertaking acid-resistant brickwork in tanks where gunpowder was distilled.

The proud Seddon horses were sent over to Europe to assist the war effort and all day-to-day activity was based around the need to support the country in this time of turmoil.

Despite Britain's victory, the after-effects of the war meant there was little to celebrate after 1918. Opportunities were scarce and the massive number of fatalities among men in their prime held the country back.

As Britain fought to recover some degree of normality after the Armistice, George Seddon travelled to Ireland to secure the services of navvies to work on the site of a spinning mill at Howe Bridge, Atherton. Slowly, business was to get back on track.

A Growing Project List

As a new decade emerged, December 17th, 1920 marked a major milestone in the Seddon brothers' business and the entire Seddon story – with the formation of a Limited company, G & J Seddon Limited. The first meeting of the Directors was held on January 3rd 1921, with George Seddon (Chairman), John Seddon and Mr Jim Grundy (Secretary).

All successful businesses have a unique selling point and for the Seddon brothers it was their skill in brickwork that formed the backbone of the company's expansion.

The anti-corrosion brickwork used in the munitions industry was transferred to the world-famous Lancashire mills, where chemical tanks were built to house the dyes.

St Paul's Peel School, Little Hulton 1906

Rope lashings and wooden pole scaffolding can be seen on this building site. Today high-visibility vests and hard hats have replaced these builders' uniforms of crisp white aprons and flat caps. The school was built near St Paul's Peel Church, on Manchester Road, where both George and John Seddon were great patrons. John was a churchwarden and chorister for 37 years at the church.

Other projects in the early 1920s included the construction of a chemical works in Walkden and, in June 1922, shares in this company were purchased by George and John. Also, in November 1922, G & J Seddon purchased shares in Howe Bridge Cotton Spinning Limited, for whom they were doing a considerable amount of work.

Major projects in Bolton carried out by Seddon included a new theatre, where the company was further able to demonstrate its brickwork skills in an ornate style, as well as work on the new Bolton Town Hall.

Manchester Road Develops

Around the mid to late 1920s, properties were constructed on the Manchester Road site, to accommodate the Seddon family as well as their business. Three houses were built, properties where George and John Seddon, together with Company Secretary, Jim Grundy, lived.

These buildings were to form the axis of the company's operations. Each housed the families of the three men, whilst offices built in basements underneath provided the accommodation for their business. At these homes, George Seddon and his wife raised one daughter and one son. John Seddon and his wife, Eliza Ellen, raised three sons and four daughters.

John and Eliza's three sons, Ernest, Jonas and Frank went on to join the family business.

Horse Power In Its Hey Day

Many pictures from the early days of Seddon show horses proudly and immaculately turned out. Often pictured at Whit Walks – the traditional processions which were an important part of life in Lancashire – the horses seemed to play a pivotal role in the social and economic fabric of the business.

This picture shows a traditional Whit Procession along Manchester Road in Little Hulton. The first house on the left is Jim Grundy's, the house next door with offices under was John Seddon's home. George Seddon's home, which also had offices under, is not shown.

Throughout the entire Seddon story, there remains a strong focus on the importance of family life. In the company's early days, that fact is reflected in these two pictures here, as people of all ages were photographed taking to the streets of Little Hulton for the important Whit Walk Procession. The horse stands proud in its fine harness and regalia.

Whit Walk Procession G & J Seddon cart – circa 1920

Horsepower peaked in the 1920s with 28 horses kept in stables at Seddon's Manchester Road site. The horses worked hard for their corn, having to make the journey from Little Hulton to brickworks at Stockport several times a day – averaging a journey of almost 70 miles in total.

As the bricks were loaded up the horses would tuck into a feed given in a traditional-style nosebag. Despite the arduous work the horses did, their glossy coats and well-upholstered rumps reflected the fact they received the best of care to enable them to perform their demanding jobs.

Mechanisation took its toll in the 1930s and the horses were replaced by the popular motor vehicles, which had started to sweep the country. Company records show the last horse was purchased by G & J Seddon for £41 10s in July 1928. The value placed on the horses was considerable when this price is compared to the fact that in the same year, two cottages in Manchester Road were purchased for £380.

Jonas Seddon, second son of John Seddon Senior, recalled

that his Uncle George travelled from one contract to another initially in a horse and trap and later on a motorbike with sidecar attached.

The Seddon Yard In Little Hulton In The 1930s

The Seddon premises housed a lime pit, stables, garages and a range of outbuildings and stores, which formed the hub of the business.

In the late 1930s, a young John Seddon, son of Ernest Seddon, remembers the adventures afforded at the site. As a three-year-old he would venture out each day, in a uniform of green overalls, to start his 'work' at the blacksmiths, helping to pump the bellows.

Then he would assist in the garage, where it was possible to get really oily. The lime pit at the far corner of the site was off limits to the youngster due to the hazardous nature of this area, but the nearby mortar pan was to provide interest. A mortar mixer man, blessed with a rich singing voice - which saw him perform in the Hallé Choir – often sang to the tune of 'Men of Harlech'

I'm The Man For Mixing Mortar Four and 20 bags a Quarter I'm The Man For Mixing Mortar In John Seddon's Yard

Young John's pay for his 'work' was three halfpennies, and his first pay packet was presented to him by Arthur Wood, who went on to become chief clerk and cashier at G & J Seddon Limited.

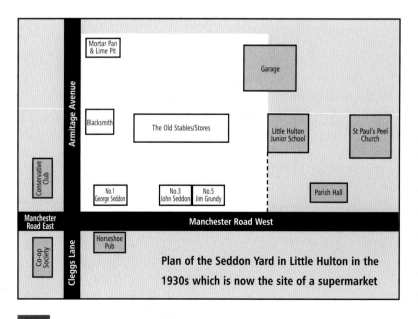

Plan of the Seddon Yard in Little Hulton in the 1930s which is now the site of a supermarket

A Diverse Business

The growing client list and specialities of G & J Seddon are reflected in the advert.

Established 1897.   *Contractors to H.M. Government.*

G. & J. SEDDON LTD.

(Directors :—G. R. SEDDON, J. SEDDON, J. D. GRUNDY)

EXCAVATORS, DRAINERS, CONCRETORS BRICKLAYERS, GENERAL CONTRACTORS AND DEALERS IN BUILDING MATERIALS

G. & J. SEDDON, LTD. CARRIED OUT the Demolition, Excavating, Draining, Reinforced Concreting, and the Brickwork for the general Reconstructing of this Theatre.

········ □ ········

We *specialise in* Churches, Schools, Public Offices, Mills, Dwelling Houses, Mansions, and everything from a Fire back to a Cotton Spinning Mill or Warehouse.

Some Recent Contracts include :

SALFORD CORPORATION : New Bus Garage and Tramsheds, New School, Lower Kersal, New Baths and Public Wash-houses.

MANCHESTER CORPORATION : Extensions Bradford Road Gasworks, New Gas Works Buildings, New Roads, and Housing Schemes at Partington Gas Works.

HOUSING SCHEMES at Farnworth, Tyldesley, Atherton, Clifton & Kersley Coal Co., Ltd.

New Townley's Hospital Extension.   New Church of St. Richards, Atherton.

Bolton Co-operative Society's New Bakery, Kay Street.

New Rose Hill Congregational Church & School, Bolton.

Extensions to Garfield Mills, Cannon Street, Bolton. Moor Mills, Parrot Street. Bolton Infirmary and scores of others.

Consult Seddon's for anything and everything in the Building Trade.

5 & 7 Manchester Road West

LITTLE HULTON, Near Bolton.

Telephone : 185 Farnworth (2 lines)   *Telegrams :* "Seddon Bros., Little Hulton.

Ernest Seddon's Wedding 1931

The Manchester Road homes even made it on to the wedding pictures of Ernest and Dora Seddon.

Strikes, Depression And Moves Further Afield

The First World War hit hard, but social and economic life was affected by a series of other factors in its aftermath that made conditions tough.

Of particular note, The General Strike of 1926 was a difficult and distressing time. Little Hulton was a mining village and many villagers had no income during the strike. To try and help the situation G & J Seddon employed the miners to construct homes that could be sold at a later date, when the nation's fortunes took an upturn. This proved the correct decision to take – and provided the men with a wage during a lean period when others found that if they did not work, they did not eat.

A more personal blow followed, with the death of George Seddon on the 23rd September 1928. For his funeral, the Works closed as the family and workers joined forces to mourn a man of extraordinary determination, enterprise and spirit.

For John, this was an incredibly difficult time and he never truly recovered from the effect of losing a brother who had been the centre of his life for as long as he could remember. However, no doubt bolstered by the memory of his brother's strength and substance, John worked hard during a difficult time to keep the business on track.

In October 1928, John was appointed Chairman and his eldest son, Ernest, then 23, was asked to assist his father and to take up the position of Travelling Foreman. Later John's

other sons, Jonas and Frank, also followed their elder brother into the business.

The Great Depression that plunged the world into desperation and chaos also took its toll on life in this corner of Lancashire in the 1930s. It was during this time that the company decided to look beyond the Red Rose county for more work.

Cups And Mortar

A contract signed in August 1935 to complete construction work to properties in Meir, Stoke-on-Trent, was to become a major turning point in Seddon's history.

This project – taking over works from another company that had ceased trading – was to sow the seeds for the eventual formation of Seddon (Stoke) Limited. A main contractor in Manchester was initially approached to take on the work but had declined the offer and suggested G & J Seddon as an alternative. The Little Hulton builders jumped at the chance to carry out work further south.

At that time, similarities existed between the Bolton and Stoke-on-Trent landscapes. Both were dominated by works housing their world-famous manufacturing skills – Lancashire with its cotton mills and Stoke its pottery industry. The coal

A young Jonas Seddon on board a Seddon cart at Little Hulton

A lasting reminder of the first project Seddon carried out in Stoke-on-Trent, at Meir, where Seddon Road was named after the company's involvement in building homes in the area in the 1930s.

mines, which George and John knew so well in Lancashire, were also in abundance in this part of Staffordshire.

For G & J Seddon, the challenge, after securing the works at Meir, was to find a way to get a foot on the ladder across the rest of the city for their business.

This challenge was to be met head-on by the young Ernest Seddon - appointed to the Board of Directors in 1930 – and already showing an inheritance of the attributes that had enabled his Father John and Uncle George to prosper.

The Right Move

Throughout the mid 1930s, Ernest Seddon continued to live in Little Hulton, where his wife Dora kept house for the family, and he made regular visits to Stoke to manage operations.

The journey was made in an open-topped Crossley car, which reflected the changing times of the era, replacing the horse and cart as the transport of choice.

One night a week, Ernest would stay in Staffordshire, at The Borough Arms Hotel in Newcastle-under-Lyme, before handing out wages the following day. He made it his personal job to ensure that the right man was paid the right rate for the right hours.

The expansion of work in and around North Staffordshire meant that Ernest and his family left Little Hulton in 1939, to live in the Cheshire town of Congleton, a mid-way point between Stoke and Bolton.

Some men from Little Hulton followed and many were to work for years in Stoke-on-Trent, on a variety of projects.

Cheer And Woe In Chell

Ernest Seddon was set for a major breakthrough in Stoke with a contract awarded just before the Second World War, to build 1,100 homes in Chell, an area of the Potteries close to the town of Burslem, in the north of the city.

The objective was to make a £1.50 profit per house, and in today's money the contract would be worth £100 million. Clearly this was a project that would transform the company's entire standing.

Work on-site was hard and the hours long. A second cousin of Ernest's, Arthur Seddon, was a tough site manager. A number of labourers and bricklayers cycled to Chell from Congleton, pedalling many miles before starting work at 7.30am, then facing the same ride home at 6pm.

On one occasion a man mounted his bike with such vigour after finishing his day's work that Arthur turned to him and said: "Don't come back to work here tomorrow; if you can get on a bicycle like that with so much energy, you've not worked hard enough for me here today." Another man, who ran at the end of the day to catch the open-topped truck that used to collect and drop off Seddon workers in Hanley, was also accused of not delivering enough energy on-site by Arthur.

Times were tough, but men were glad of the work and the distraction from what was looming around the corner, as Hitler's rise to power created a dangerous situation in Europe.

Another war was coming, and when it was declared, the building at Chell was to stop, with 100 properties completed. The contract signed to build 1,100 homes was cancelled and many of the men were forced to swap the tools of their trade for weapons - the country had a bigger job to do.

The first Stoke Office –
one rented room in a
property in Brook
Street, off Glebe Street,
Stoke, was the site of
the first office for
Seddon in the city. It
was opened in the
1930s due to its
proximity to a bank, to
access cash for payday.

A view of Meir in the
1930s when Seddon
were building new
homes in the area.

Photo courtesy of The
Potteries Museum & Art
Gallery

These three photographs paint a fascinating picture of the construction industry in the 1930s in Stoke-on-Trent. Taken at Trent Vale, they show work to build homes around Keelings Drive – possibly Forber Road or Sutton Drive.

Seddon worked in the area at this time, although it is not known if these pictures are of the company's workers.

Photos courtesy of the Potteries Museum and Art Gallery.

Chapter 2 Building a City

The Second World War And Its Aftermath

For Ernest Seddon, working at the 'coal face' with his team of men day in and day out – one of the most upsetting aspects of the Second World War was seeing so many of his respected team pack up their tools and prepare to mobilise across the world for the fight.

Ernest had hoped to serve with the Army's Staffordshire Regiment – but his skills as a builder rather than a soldier were called upon by King and country. His role in the war was to remain on home soil, under the command of the War Office.

Working at a time when people were trying hard to cope with food shortages, air raids and fears of a telegram from overseas bringing news of death, it was no easy task.

Seddon was put on War Directions by the War Office, with projects including the building of Anderson Shelters at key strategic locations to protect local residents. Underground reinforced shelters were also built in the playgrounds of schools. Much of this work was centred around Stoke-on-Trent, in particular in the south of the city.

Another major project was construction work on airfields for the Air Ministry in Northern Ireland. This vital work, creating false dug-outs and other obstacles, was devised to prevent enemy forces landing in the United Kingdom. On a weekly basis, Ernest Seddon would fly in blacked-out military aeroplanes for the journey across the Irish Sea – to avoid being detected and targeted by the enemy – in order to carry out this work.

As the war took hold, work was also directed towards repairing bomb damage and rebuilding the shattered ruins of major cities, including London, Coventry and Cardiff.

Such was the scale of the work involved in rebuilding these bombed areas that Frank Seddon, younger brother of Ernest, temporarily moved to Cardiff from the North West to help restore the area.

Getting The Nation Back On Its Feet

The process of getting back to normal after the war was a difficult one, both physically and mentally, for all involved. In terms of the physical aspect, the construction industry was boosted by the fact building workers were given demobilisation priority after the war. The emotional cost was less easy to measure – but to see men back at home and back at work could only be a heartening sight.

Work soon started at the full throttle pace seen in Chell prior to war breaking out. This time the location was still North Staffordshire, but in the Beasley and Bradwell areas of Newcastle-under-Lyme, building council estate homes and some Airey houses – a type of pre-fabricated property.

Men dug all the foundations by hand – and the family focus at the heart of the company once again started to develop. One family of skilled drainage and foundation men would work in a line overseen by their father. He would aim a well-placed implement at any member of the line – family or not – seen to be slacking.

The Airey homes all had wooden fences to keep their grounds safe and secure. George Allen, who went on to become Seddon Senior Contracts Manager, earned the title of 'fencer in chief' for his carpentry skills.

Ernest Seddon

At Beasley and Bradwell, the company had 100 men working on 400 homes – this would be the modern equivalent of a £20 million contract in today's money.

Seddon builders then made their way to Wood Lane and Sun Street in Etruria, as well as other locations across North Staffordshire. Times were hard – rations saw one week's measure of food for an adult fit on a five-inch plate. Furthermore, all work was being carried out manually – the diggers and other associated machinery were still in their infancy and only very slowly introduced on to construction sites. Such conditions meant the construction workers of this era were a strong, lean breed to be reckoned with – and they needed all the strength they could muster as the 1940s were left behind to make way for the brighter, more positive – and very busy – 1950s.

CITY OF STOKE-ON-TRENT

HOUSING
1919 TO 1955

Cover of a brochure which explains the housing plan for Bentilee and other areas in Stoke-on-Trent.

Jack Hulme, who headed Seddon's painting operations for many years. A brilliant estimator he could work out a job on the back of a cigarette packet. He was the major influence in the painting department throughout the 1950s, 60s and into the 70s.

Painting a Brighter Future

Seddon's work was not just limited to building projects. The company's work in painting and maintenance had been going from strength to strength before war broke out. Just before the conflict, there was a contract to paint more than 1,000 properties in the Burslem area of Stoke-on-Trent. Post-war, the painters had a flood of work – although rationing and shortages meant innovative methods were needed to ensure materials were available to carry out projects for a number of years after the conflict ended. Jack Hulme, who headed up the painting operations, had his own secret formula for painting ceilings – lime wash and Irish moss. The lime was 'slaked' on site – a term meaning to heat and crumble by treatment with water. Workers remember lime pits being built to accommodate burnt limestone delivered from Buxton. It was placed in a lime pit area and water added to the stone. As steam rose from the slab, a milky-white slurry would run off – and this was made into the lime wash.

The moss was then sourced by Jack Hulme (**pictured top left**). How this moss was obtained was kept a closely-guarded secret by Jack. The paint obtained using this method went on beautifully, but left a very distinctive – and somewhat unpleasant – smell.

As the nation geared up to meet the needs of a booming post war population, the company's next challenge was a considerable one - transforming the entire fabric of the county with a major building programme, which represented the start of a new era, not just in Staffordshire, but across Britain.

Many local authorities had a policy of buying up farms to create the space for developments to accommodate the growing population and to replace slum housing. Stoke-on-Trent was no exception and the green fields of areas known today as Blurton and Bentilee – along with other sites around the city – were soon to be transformed as part of this building programme.

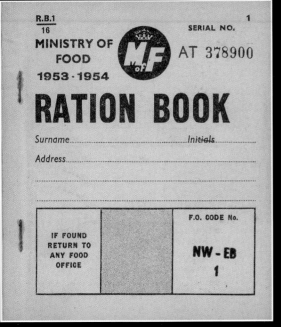

Food rations must have taken their toll on the condition of young apprentices judging by Ray Herbert's experiences in his early working days. As a 14-year-old trainee, Ray **(pictured below)** remembers he and his work friends were not allowed to leave the company's yard and go on to site until they were capable of lifting a hundredweight bag of cement – by order of Ernest Seddon. Ray joined the company in the 1940s and went onto become a General Foreman. He clocked up 51 years' service with Seddon.

After being demobbed following the war, Arthur Sadler's papers stated "this man has great powers of improvisation," written by his Commanding Officer. Arthur's handyman skills were called to the fore in wartime, where he made props for the entertainment of the troops. Despite being a Potter born and bred, Arthur **(pictured above in 2006 and right at his wedding in 1940)** was posted to the Army's historic Black Watch Regiment and wore the traditional uniform for his wedding. Arthur had worked for Seddon before the Second World War and came back to the company once he was demobbed. Describing his return, Arthur said: "I was thrilled to be back and to settle down and have my mates nearby again." After the war, Arthur continued his association with his Scottish regiment and was an active member of the Black Watch Association in Staffordshire. He retired from Seddon aged 75.

Workers familiar with the military environment from the war effort and National Service, which was introduced afterwards, were more than able to cope with the demands for a smart turnout in their work with Seddon. All bricklayers had to have immaculate workboots at the start of the week each Monday morning.

George Grocott (pictured above in 2006), served with the Royal Navy in the war before joining Seddon. He remembers under their pristine overalls, painters always wore a collar and tie. George, who is pictured left in his Navy uniform, once sent an apprentice home for having a dirty neck. George worked as a painter and was a senior contracts manager for Seddon. In total he worked for the company for 40 years.

Jozef Witkowski - who joined Seddon as a Contracts Manager after the war - was a pilot in the Polish Air Force and flew Spitfires, designed by North Staffordshire's Reginald Mitchell, on a number of daring sorties. He has appeared on television and in print interviews, talking about the merits of the Spitfire and his war time experiences.

Jozef pictured at home in Stoke-on-Trent in 2006. He worked for the company for 26 years.

Air raid shelters such as this at Woodcocks Well Primary School in Mow Cop, on the Staffordshire and Cheshire border, were a common sight. Seddon built a number of these structures during wartime.

From the 1940s and for decades afterwards, Seddon played a massive part in the construction of buildings at RAF Stafford. One of their earliest jobs there was building concrete barrack block accommodation. Prisoners of War helped to build this and – when they were allowed back to their native lands after the war - a number decided to stay with Seddon instead. The last German POWs working on the unit left in 1947, but among those who stayed was Hans Mattern. Hans, who is believed to have served as a German tank driver during the war, was a popular and well-respected member of the Seddon team, who was noted for his ability to drive any sort of excavating equipment.

Picture courtesy of RAF Stafford

Here Hans (far left) is pictured with Seddon colleague Bill Rockey in the late 1960s/early 1970s. The young lady in the picture is believed to be a relative of Hans.

Hans was well known across the company for his lunch, which consisted of half a loaf of bread, a jam jar full of dripping and an onion each day.

Hazel Taylor **(pictured opposite)** in 2006 with her wartime identity book, worked for Seddon during the conflict. Her family construction company, Maddock Brothers of Audley, in North Staffordshire, was temporarily wound down during the war years as all the men in the business were called up into battle. She saw an advert for an administration assistant placed by Seddon and went to work at the Stoke office, off Glebe Street.

She remembers projects including the construction of Nissen huts in Hassell Green and Delamere in Cheshire, and general work at Oswestry Hospital in Shropshire, which cared for military personnel injured in the war effort. As well as working at Stoke, Hazel was sent for a spell up to G & J Seddon's Little Hulton office, where she remembers catching the train into Piccadilly Station and making her way across Manchester during the height of the bombing raids. Hazel said: *'The blackouts in winter were the worst aspect, travelling home in the dark with little light, carrying a gas mask. It was a difficult time, but the people were very nice. When I worked at G & J Seddon, I lodged with Mr Tildesley and his family, and they were friendly. At the office, in Manchester Road West, there was a telephone switchboard system located in rooms underground, which I liked to use.'*

'At Seddon in Stoke, I worked with Ernest Seddon, who was always a gentleman and incredibly busy. When he came into the office at Glebe Street, it would always be a rush to get whatever he needed. Also, there was Mr WJ Davis, Arnold Hadley and a lady called Dolly. The wages were worked out on great big sheets and would take ages to do. On Friday

mornings we went to the bank and had to go at different times to deter robbers.'

'During the war, we moved to Duke Street in Fenton. At that time, the offices were little more than a row of cottages.'

'Summer-times were pleasant. At Delamere, I would sometimes travel on the workmen's bus to do the administration work on site, and wages were paid through a little window from the site office.'

'When I was asked to work at G & J Seddon, I would travel from Stoke to Piccadilly Station, and then walk across the city to catch a bus to Little Hulton. I would work all week and travel home on Saturday morning, returning on Monday morning. When we drew into Manchester, we often could

Seddon receptionist Katie Middleton, a neighbour of Hazel Taylor (pictured opposite), who discovered the pensioner had worked for the company during the war.

Hazel Taylor, pictured in 2006, who worked for Seddon during the Second World War.

not get into the station due to the bombings. Houses were destroyed and there were bricks and other material all over the floor. I would see this and just run for the tram or bus to Little Hulton as quickly as I could. We all pulled together. The times were hard and we saw many of the men called-up to fight, but we kept going. Mr Jonas Seddon would bring a smile with his singing. He liked to sing and keep spirits up.'

Despite the hardships of the war, Hazel enjoyed her time with Seddon and eventually went back to her family's firm when the war ended. Her story only came to light when Seddon receptionist, Katie Middleton, **(pictured left)** told Hazel, who is her neighbour, that she had started work with the company.

The war years also marked a significant event in the history of the Seddon company. In 1942, a plot of land comprising of 360 square yards – fronting the old tramway in Fenton – was purchased at 4s.6d per square yard. In time this site – now known as Duke Street – was to become the home of Seddon (Stoke) Ltd.

Picture courtesy of www.thepotteries.org

Working for the War Office, Seddon would have been involved not only in the construction of air raid shelters, but also making safe bomb damaged properties such as this situated in the north of Stoke-on-Trent. The city was not severely affected by bomb damage, although there were a number of buildings destroyed and lives lost in enemy raids.

Picture courtesy of The Potteries Museum and Art Gallery

WALPAMUR Quality Paints

bring colour before you wherever you live, in town or country, in large house or small. Colour adds to the gaiety of life and those famous paints ensure its durability. Use Walpamur Water Paint on walls and ceilings—you can buy a special quality for exterior work—Duradio, the easy to apply, quick to dry Super Enamel Paint for a long-lasting high gloss inside and out, and Darwen Satin Finish for any room, especially kitchens and bathrooms where its enamelproof surface is ideal.

Send for shade cards and literature to
The Walpamur Co. Ltd., Darwen, Lancs.

After the war, manufactured paints became easier to obtain. One brand that was well-known in the marketplace was Walpamur. The term referring to painting as 'wallop' stems from the name Walpamur.

Chapter 3 The Start Of A New Era

Enterprise And Enthusiasm In The 1950s And 1960s.

As the country underwent a massive redevelopment programme, Seddon builders and painters would roll up their sleeves and get to grips with a clutch of large-scale contracts.

Across Britain, the 1950s marked a period of great renewal. Recovering from the hardships of the war, the country picked itself up, brushed itself off and looked straight ahead to the future with a lighter heart – the new decade marking a period of excitement with changes and challenges ahead.

Eventually, material and manpower shortages slowly became less of a challenge, but workers were still forced to adhere to food rationing for years after the war – with food limited even in to the 1950s.

On The Move

Transporting hundreds of men each day to the various work sites was an operation run with military precision. One man associated with Seddon on the move was Ken Sproston, an ex Sergeant Major who worked at the company as head of the transport department.

Today, Seddon vans can be seen the length and breadth of the country, but in the 1950s, Seddon operated its own fleet of green buses to get workers about. Along with the buses, men also travelled in canopied lorries. The canopy would offer shelter and shade against the elements for the workers and, once on site, the cover would be removed so the lorry could be used as a construction site vehicle, carrying sand, bricks and other materials.

A Seddon Bus.

While company cars and vans were few and far between compared with 21st century requirements, transport could still present problems. In 1958, directors were told that a new car was needed for the surveyor Bill Saunders, as the one he was using was obsolete, the coach BUX 793 was in need of replacement and a new van was needed to replace one smashed up in an accident.

Sad Times

In 1954, the company was saddened by the death of Mr John Seddon senior, at the age of 79. John had founded Seddon's with his brother George.

Gilbert Longworth, who was his driver, was a bearer at his funeral, along with Alec Armstrong, Paul Fletcher and Fred Seddon – all long-serving employees.

Less than twelve months earlier John Seddon senior had opened G & J Seddon's new offices in Coronation Buildings, Armitage Avenue, Little Hulton. Before the official opening, the AGM was held, where John outlined his plans for the future, saying *'he hoped he would be spared to carry on as he had done in the past. If he could get up to the office and go around the sites when the weather was suitable, he would be quite happy.'*

At the AGM, John Seddon senior also gave a philosophical view on his family business, and showed his pride in its success. He said *'he'd always thought of a building firm as a ladder – you could not stay on a rung for very long, you must go up or come down – and he was very proud his firm had gone up the ladder. He had looked forward to the opening of new offices and was to have the pleasure of officially opening the new premises later that afternoon. He concluded that he only hoped his grandsons would take as much interest in the firm as his sons - and if they did they would not go far wrong.'*

In the same decade the company's minutes go on to report that five of his grandsons were working for the business, Christopher, George, John, Michael and David.

Mr John Seddon senior, the joint founder of Seddon, with his wife Eliza Ellen, at Coronation Buildings in 1953.

A group shot at the opening of Coronation Buildings.

Fuel Concerns

International relations had an effect on business in the 1950s. The Suez Crisis led to the flow of petrol in the UK being severely affected as British and French forces launched a joint raid in 1956 on Egypt to regain control of the newly-nationalised Suez Canal. The Egyptian President Abdel Nasser responded by sinking ships in the canal and effectively closing it to shipping. By 1955, two-thirds of Europe's oil passed through the Suez, so the situation took its toll on fuel supplies in the UK.

For Seddon, large uneconomical vehicles were put into storage, and more fuel efficient transport methods sought. Ernest Seddon's powerful 30HP motor car was exchanged for a VW Beetle and motorbikes were used instead of company cars. These restrictions were in place for around 12 months until the situation in the Middle East was resolved and normal fuel supplies reintroduced.

An Important Date

1957 marks an important time in the history of Seddon, with the formation of Seddon (Stoke) Limited on the 1st February. The first meeting of Seddon (Stoke) Limited was held at Coronation Buildings in Little Hulton – the village where George and John Seddon senior had first started the family business in 1897. John Seddon senior's sons, Ernest, Jonas and Frank Seddon were all appointed Directors, and Jonas took up the role of Company Secretary. 55 Duke Street in Fenton, Stoke-on-Trent, was appointed as the registered office. Ernest Seddon was appointed Chairman.

Soon after, Mr Jack Finney was appointed a Director. Jack had joined G & J Seddon in 1936 and had been with the company continuously, apart from three to four years' war service, where he had served as an Army Officer. Before being appointed as a Director, Jack had been acting as a Contracts Manager in Stoke.

Seddon (Stoke) Limited's first contract was won from the British Transport Commission in London. Involving cleaning and painting platforms 12 to 17 at Manchester's Victoria Passenger Station, the deal was worth £7,247.6s.2d.

The British Transport Commission, along with the Air Ministry, were two of Seddon's largest customers at the time, with various works carried out on their behalf. Local authorities were also major clients – in particular Leek Urban District Council, Leek Rural District Council, City of Stoke-on-Trent, the Borough of Stafford, Newcastle-under-Lyme Rural District Council and the Borough of Newcastle-under-Lyme.

Mr Jack Finney – appointed Director of Seddon (Stoke) in 1957.

Seddon also played a part in the post-war development of the Staffordshire Moorlands. In July 1957, a contract was signed with Leek Urban District Council for houses at Windsor Drive, on the Haregate Estate in Leek, for £11,129.15s.5d. Then in the winter, a contract for one pair of "Type K" houses on the estate was received, valued at £3,178.12s.10d, before a much larger deal – of £61,925.1s.6d was received for 40 houses of "Type KUV and T."

Over the moors into Derbyshire, Seddon built properties as part of an ongoing project in the 1950s at Harpur Hill, one of the highest points in England, near to Buxton. The sheer strength of limestone underground meant foundations had to be created using explosives. The late Blaster Bates, a well-known Northern demolition expert, was called in to get to grips with the rocky environment. Unfortunately, on one occasion the blasts sent debris through electric wires, causing a power cut across the entire area. Work at Harpur Hill was called to a halt in October due to the ferocity of the region's winters, resuming in the following spring. Transport to the site was on the back of a wagon with a canvas canopy and the journey alone made it impossible for workers to keep warm in a Moorlands winter.

In 1958, Ernest Seddon reported that competition was very keen in Stoke-on-Trent – and it seemed it would be difficult to obtain work. Questions were raised over the viability of moving into the civil engineering sector and Seddon Fleischer was set up and carried out numerous civil engineering contracts, although it was closed down in the 1960s as work focused on the core areas of building and painting.

The Dragon And The White Rose Connection

1958 also marked the start of Seddon (Stoke) moving into new areas – looking north to York and west to Anglesey to continue its growth.

Jack Hulme said at a meeting that he wanted a central yard in Yorkshire to base operations. Three years later, premises were bought and the York office quickly developed into the hub of operations for painting in the north – a position that continues almost five decades later. In the early days, Jack Tierney, Herbert Blood and Fred Smith were among some of the Seddon team of Stoke men associated with the York office.

The York office – the hub of operations for painting in the North.

35

A large scale contract from the Air Ministry was secured in the 1960s for major works at RAF Valley in Anglesey and then, one year later, a contract was signed with Llangefni Urban District Council to build a six-storey block of flats at Glandwr Terrace in Llangefni for £61,361.16s.7d.

The flats at Glandwr Terrace boasted all the latest mod cons – and a room with a view. However, when a Government Minister came to open the development, he was heard to ask in hushed tones why – in an area as open and spacious as Anglesey – there had been a need to build a tower block.

The people of North Staffordshire have always had an affinity with North Wales and Seddon workers soon slotted into life on Anglesey. John Seddon junior successfully won contracts with the Air Ministry at RAF Valley and it was ongoing work for the Military in Anglesey that led to the development of a staff base in the area. To start the ball rolling, a house was purchased for Bill Saunders – the minutes of 1958 state that "there was a long term prospect in the area." Ernest and Frank Seddon had visited the region and felt Trearddur Bay was ripe for private development – although this later fell through due to drainage difficulties.

To cater for the increasing workload, a site for offices and stores was purchased from the Air Ministry. Later work was carried out to Holyhead County Secondary School, a library, swimming pool and gym, as well as a museum for Anglesey County Council - and runway work for RAF Valley. Painting work was also carried out across the island.

John Seddon then persuaded other Potteries men and their wives and families to move to Anglesey. Bill Saunders was joined by Tony Williams, Bill Scott and Dave Povey amongst others to start their own Seddon community in Anglesey. Fifteen bungalows were built on the island. Some were sold privately but the company kept a number of the properties, to provide homes for Seddon staff working in the area. Others associated with Anglesey included Roy Grocott, Ken Podmore, Harry Jones and Bert Bloor.

For eleven years, each Wednesday, John Seddon junior would travel from Stoke-on-Trent to Anglesey to arrive at 7.30am to oversee the operations of the office. This included the wages – never an easy task as, at one stage, there were 41 Welshmen on the payroll all with the surname Jones.

Anglesey was also the place of a major incident in the Seddon history – a wages theft. The story made the national newspapers at the time.

Modern homes for modern living, these flats in Llangefni, Anglesey, included every conceivable extra, fridge, television – and even a food blender.

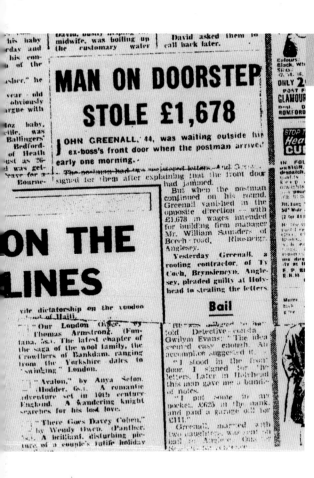

MAN ON DOORSTEP STOLE £1,678

JOHN GREENALL, 44, was waiting outside his ex-boss's front door when the postman arrived early one morning.

The postman had two registered letters. And Greenall signed for them after explaining that the front door had jammed.

But when the postman continued on his round, Greenall vanished in the opposite direction — with £1,678 in wages intended for building firm manager Mr. William Saunders, of Beech-road, Rhosneigr, Anglesey.

Yesterday Greenall, a roofing contractor, of Ty Coch, Brynsiencyn, Anglesey, pleaded guilty at Holyhead to stealing the letters.

Bail

He was alleged to have told Detective-constable Gwilym Evans: "The idea seemed easy enough. An accomplice suggested it.

"I stood in the front door, I signed for the letters. Later in Holyhead this man gave me a bundle of notes.

"I put some in my pocket, £625 in the bank, and paid a garage bill for £111."

Greenall, married with two daughters, was sent on bail to Anglesey Quarter Sessions.

ON THE LINES

...vile dictatorship on the voodoo coast of Haiti.

"Our London Office," by Thomas Armstrong. (Fontana, 5s.). The latest chapter of the saga of the Crowthers of Bankdam, ranging from the Yorkshire dales to "swinging" London.

"Avalon," by Anya Seton. (Hodder, 6s.). A romantic adventure set in 10th century England. A wandering knight searches for his lost love.

"There Goes Davey Cohen," by Wendy Owen. (Panther, ...s.). A brilliant, disturbing picture of a couple's Isle of Wight holiday.

Cheshire and the company was chosen for the project. Valued at £774,715 9s 1d – this was, at the time, the largest ever contract signed by Seddon (Stoke) Ltd. The work was completed in 1960 and Ernest Seddon thanked Jack Finney personally for his work to ensure the project went smoothly. The new building was a source of considerable pride among Seddon staff, and a bus trip was even laid on to take workers and their families to see the finished development.

Despite this success, around this time it was agreed work might need to be carried out further afield and meetings were to be arranged with executives every three months so they would be aware they might have to work away from home. At this time a policy of building private housing was also agreed – subject to being able to find suitable land, with funding provided by G & J Seddon.

The painting side of the business was busy, but discussions were held over the possibility of reducing the number of employed staff working in building – in areas including excavating, concreting and brickwork.

Another theft was never solved – that of the Holyhead scaffolding. A massive amount of metalwork was taken from the town, but Seddon staff were unable to work out who was stealing it or where it went.

A Busman's Holiday

Seddon (Stoke) received a massive boost in August 1959. ICI wanted new offices in Winnington at Northwich,

A staff trip with a difference - on the bus for a visit to see the new ICI building at Winnington, Northwich.

Built by Seddon, ICI's Brunner House in Winnington, Northwich. Ted Cheadle managed the contract on site, which was one of a number of large scale prestigious projects he carried out for Seddon throughout the 1950s, 60s and 70s.

you some difficult work.' He remained determined to join the building trade and, before leaving school, signed his apprenticeship papers as a trainee bricklayer.

Tea Breaks And Falling Temperatures

Matters relating to two major issues in the British construction industry – tea-breaks and the weather – came to a head in the early 1960s. Ernest Seddon reported on August 22, 1961, that he had concerns over the October 1961 Working Rules Agreement. He felt it might lead to trouble because 'it affected tea-breaks.' The Agreement was to put an end to more leisurely breaks that the industry had started to enjoy. Such was the concern over the issue that a meeting was held at the Midland Hotel in Manchester to 'alleviate concerns and iron out potential problems.'

Much more serious was the Big Freeze of 1962 and 1963, which led to Seddon's work on site being halted for three months. The whole firm was closed as frost bit down more than two feet into the ground. Foremen were put on watch duty to protect the vacant building sites and hundreds of men were laid off. Apprentices – who could not be laid off - were found work that was not affected by the frost. An insight into how serious the situation was is given by John Seddon, who remembers going up on site to Bentilee and seeing all the damage caused by the weather, the men out of work - and the wage bills still going out for apprentices and foremen. He thought at that stage the company might have been forced out of business.

Joining The Board

John Seddon was made a Director of Seddon (Stoke) in March 1960, making the move from bricklayer and foreman to the boardroom, working in an industry he had set his heart on from an early age. At Shrewsbury School, where he was a boarding pupil, John's housemaster had plans for the youngster to go to Oxford University. At a careers event, John and other pupils had assembled in the school's main hall prior to a visit from the professions and Government departments. When the headmaster had introduced the visitors, he asked the pupils if any had plans for their future careers. John raised his hand and said: 'I want to be a builder Sir.' Looking down at the young man, the headmaster – disappointed that one of his pupils was not pursuing a career on the academic route - boomed: 'I've seen enough of you today Seddon, go back to your room and tell your housemaster to give

On The Up

These matters were overcome and Ernest Seddon reported to the Board in the company minutes of April 1963 that *'there were plenty of enquiries and we have taken advantage of them.'* He went on to say: *'The number of men engaged was in the region of 600 and was likely to increase this next few months, and we were getting enquiries which we had to refuse because the Directors felt it was no use mushrooming any growth, it was better to go steadily as in the past, and have patience and be quite sure before we took contracts on that we had someone of our own staff to look after them, people we had brought up and in whom we had confidence.'*

One year later, business continued to improve, with Ernest reporting his pleasure that the *'company had really got up on its feet and we can look forward with confidence to the future.'*

The Bennett Precinct
Picture courtesy of the Potteries Museum and Art Gallery

A Fear of Heights

In April 1963, Seddon started work on the contract for Longton Shopping Centre, which became the Bennett Precinct – with Ted Cheadle the site manager. Years later, sometime after work had been completed, the clock within the development, which stood around 30 feet high, stopped working and Seddon went on-site together with various other parties involved in the project to see what repairs were needed. Harry Richards represented Seddon at the meeting. He watched as a clock repairman mounted some ladders to climb to the tower, in order to establish what work needed to be carried out. Unfortunately the clock repairer had a fear of heights and – in full view of the party on the ground – he had to abandon his trip halfway up and return to more solid footings. Harry had full sympathy for the man – he too had an extreme fear of heights and, as a surveyor, would dread climbing on to roofs.

Harry Richards, pictured in the centre of this photograph with Phil Brooke, left, and Ken Robinson, right .
Picture courtesy of Harry Richards

Painting projects abounded in the 1950s at hospitals and other public buildings. This plan from the Walpamur Company – now Akzo Nobel Decorative Coatings Limited – detailed a new colour scheme for the Main Ward (Number 18) at St Edward's Hospital in Cheddleton. For decades, Seddon worked across St Edward's, carrying out painting work.

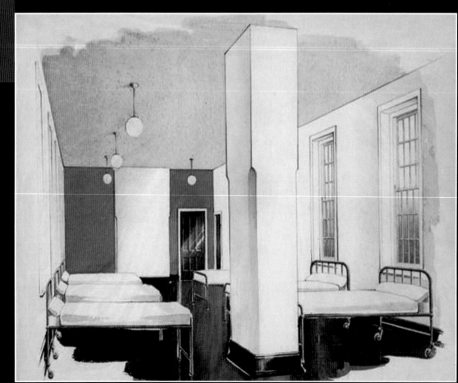

Built in the 1950s and 1960s, Bentilee, was one of Europe's largest council housing estates. Seddon carried out a number of contracts to build hundreds of homes on the site. Seddon was also one of a number of builders working in a co-operative to support the construction of the Harold Clowes Centre on the estate, named in honour of Sir Harold Clowes who was a key figure in the redevelopment of Stoke-on-Trent after the Second World War.

Sir Harold Clowes invited all builders in North Staffordshire who were involved in the major council housing programme to Stoke Town Hall in 1955, to celebrate their work.

Links With The Potters

In April 1968, Ernest Seddon signed a contract for £40, 512
10s for the second stage of a stand at Stoke City Football
Club at the Victoria Ground. The work cemented the start of
a long-term relationship between Seddon and the football
club, which had begun in the 1950s with the first phase of
the construction of the stand.

**This advert taken from Stoke City Football Club's official
programme, dated Saturday, 24th January, 1959, includes
an advert from Seddon (Stoke) - who are described as
'main contractors for the building of our new stand.' This
work relates to the first phase of the new stand project.**
Picture of the programme courtesy of Stoke City Football Club

The first million pound deal for Seddon (Stoke), a contract to build a factory for Harrison Mayer.

Hitting A Million

John Seddon was made Managing Director of Seddon (Stoke) in 1968. The year also marked the first million pound deal for Seddon. Harrison Mayer gave the company a contract valued at £1,017,422 11s 6d to build a new factory in Stoke-on-Trent – in the Meir area.

Another contract was secured in the 1960s for the Accident Unit, an operating theatre and ward block at the North Staffordshire Royal Infirmary. The contract, with Birmingham Regional Hospital Board, was for £308,745.13s.8d.

Powering Ahead

Despite the scale of projects undertaken during this time, and the sheer amount of manpower involved, construction was a far slower process compared with today's building industry. Innovative fast-track building processes and advanced plant and machinery have dramatically reduced construction programmes in modern times, but for Seddon men working in the 1950s, into the 1960s, work was truly 'hands-on.'

As a result, a building site could become a fairly permanent working environment. Due to the large scale of these projects, workers on site would often work for long periods of time at a single location. Contract Managers in particular could spend a decade on just one or two sites, with individual programmes running for years and years.

Len Walker (pictured on page 46) worked for Seddon for more than 30 years, but much of this time was spent on just three sites – RAF Cosford, RAF Stafford and Longton Hall Farm, the private housing development in Blurton.

Len Walker, pictured in 2006.

On site at RAF Cosford.

Drainage needed careful consideration at the Longton Hall project in Blurton. As a result, a dedicated pre-cast factory was set up by Seddon to build the culverts for the site. The pre-cast factory, which was situated near to the Blurton site, also made lintels for the openings of doors and windows.

Picture courtesy of Bill Rockey

Private Housing

Seddon Properties was created in 1961, and the minutes of the Directors' meeting describe its primary function as being *'to take over from the building companies and develop to advantage such parts of their developments as needed special consideration, such as sites for homes, shops, public houses, petrol stations or flats. The properties developed could then either be sold, leased or rented.'* The initial Directors were Jonas Seddon, the Chairman, John Seddon and Andrew Brown.

Across Staffordshire and Cheshire, land was purchased and developed at sites including;

Longton Hall Farm, Blurton
Wedgwood Farm, near to Chell
Bank Farm, Holmes Chapel
Sutton
Chelford
Packmoor
Tytherington
Henshall Hall

Hundreds of privately-owned homes were built at these sites, with work on site continuing for decades after the 1960s.

In August 1963 there was a discussion regarding the first phase of the Longton Hall project at Blurton – one of the largest private housing projects undertaken by Seddon - and the type of houses to be built. At the meeting it was suggested that these might be similar to the type built at Poynton. Those directors who had not seen the Poynton houses were to call on their return to Stoke to see the design for themselves.

Homes at Bank Farm in Holmes Chapel, built by Seddon.

A Learning Environment

Snow on site at Birches Head, near Hanley, where Seddon were building a Roman Catholic school in the 1960s.
Picture courtesy of Mr Jozef Witkowski

This picture shows building work taking place at Stoke-on-Trent College's Moorland Road site in Burslem.
Picture courtesy of Mr Jozef Witkowski

Flying High

Although Seddon was on-site at RAF Stafford during the war, it was the 1960s when a massive amount of work was completed. The Sergeants' and Airmen's Mess, the NAAFI building, barrack blocks and a new church were just some of the buildings constructed.

The company's work did not just focus on RAF Stafford. Across in Shropshire, Seddon also undertook major work at RAF Cosford and stations at Tern Hill and Shawbury. The work for the RAF also extended beyond the West Midlands, including the North East and North Wales.

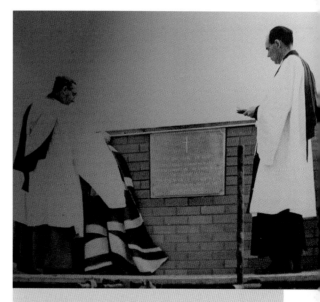

The Bishop of Lichfield, Dr AS Reeve dedicating the new church, St Chad's, in February 1961. Seddon built the church.
Picture courtesy of RAF Stafford

Princess Margaret visited the Seddon-built NAAFI building in 1959 during an official visit to RAF Stafford, one year after its opening.
Picture courtesy of RAF Stafford

The boiler house chimney in the background of this picture at RAF Stafford took its toll on workers at Seddon. The entire structure had to be built by hand – there was no crane or hydraulic lifting equipment in use at this time. Workers recall having muscles on their muscles due to the strenuous nature of the works involved.

Picture courtesy of Gordon Fishwick

First drinks in the new Sergeants' Mess in April 1960, which was built by Seddon.

Picture courtesy of RAF Stafford

Reaching New Levels

Billed by the local evening newspaper, The Sentinel, as a 'Skyscraper Village,' the construction of Bucknall Flats created a great deal of excitement in the 1960s.

Innovative methods saw much of the building arrive on site as pre-cast concrete units. Workers were constructing the flats as the 1966 World Cup was played out. There was no time off to catch-up with television or radio reports of England's progress - although with the contest held on home soil, many of the games were played around traditional British working hours. At these flats, Ernest Seddon donated a public garden and contributed to the bridge which links the road between the development.

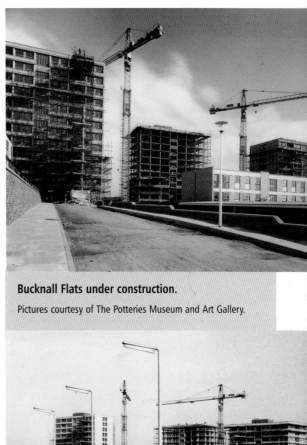

Bucknall Flats under construction.
Pictures courtesy of The Potteries Museum and Art Gallery.

The vogue for high-rise living in Stoke-on-Trent also included blocks of flats in Blurton and Honeywall, Penkhull, constructed for the local authority.
Pictured left are high rise flats in Blurton, Pedley Court and Robinson Court, built by Seddon.
Picture courtesy of The Potteries Museum and Art Gallery.

Scaling the heights, Seddon at Bucknall Flats
The Sentinel's headline announces the new
development. Newspaper cuttings courtesy of The Sentinel.

The official opening
phase two of the Buck
New-road urban rene
scheme took place to-
The Lord Mayor of St
on-Trent, Alderman
Moran, is seen with
Harry Brown, Chai
of the Housing Comm
who performed the
ing ceremony, Mr.
Plant, left, City Arch
and Mr. Ernest Sedd

Second to none

The scheme had been carried out by a consortium of local builders led by Seddon (Stoke), Ltd., in a spirit of co-operation which involved the City Architect's and all departments of the corporation.

The flats were of standards advised by the Parker-Morris Committee, and accommodation ranged from bed-sitters to -three - bedroom family homes. The standard of workmanship was second to none in the country.

"Above all it is the opinion of all who have worked here, or have visited the site, that it has been a happy one, devoid of the conflicts that unfortunately seem to beset others of this size in other areas," Mr. Brown said.

Referring to the environmental planning, Mr. Brown said the Housing Committee had set a very high standard in the landscaping and amenities within the scheme.

"This has been a team effort from start to finish," he concluded. "Members of the team are rewarded by the results of their efforts seen to-day, and in the general satisfaction of the people they have housed."

The Lord Mayor, Alderman A. Moran, who presided at the handing-over ceremony, said the scheme marked yet another milestone in the modernisation of Stoke-on-Trent.

Mr. Ernest Seddon, representing Seddons (Stoke) Ltd., handed over a personal dona-

£1.7m. city 'skyscraper village' is completed

Hanley's £1,785,000 "skyscraper village" —the Bucknall New-road urban renewal scheme—was formally completed to-day.

With its six 12-storey blocks of flats as the most prominent feature, the scheme, built on the site of cleared slums, is the largest of its type carried out by Stoke-on-Trent Corporation.

At a handing-over ceremony of the £1 million second phase of the contract, the Housing Chairman, Mr. Harry Brown, said the scheme would make a substantial contribution to the redevelopment of Hanley; which was recognised as the city centre.

And he gave a hint that despite recent criticism of tall-storey flats development more may be on the way.

"Certain city councillors favour extensive flats development and others are against it," he said. "It is not strictly true that I am against flats. I supported this scheme and I will support others where flats are necessary. I will not support flats where there is no demand—and that includes Tunstall."

Mr. Brown said the Bucknall New-road scheme fulfilled the requirements of the City Council in revitalising an area close to the most important shopping centre in the North West Midlands.

£1.7m. 'VILLAGE' IS COMPLETED

Continued from Page 1

tion of an open air "lounge" with seats for old people.

Thanking him, Mr. Brown said the roofed-in structure commanded views over an area which were once seen from the former Hanley "rocks."

Mr. Brown was thanked by his Vice-Chairman, Mr. R. Southern.

Other contractors involved in the second phase of the scheme were G. A. Poole Ltd., W. Leake and Company, Ltd., Naylor and Nutt Ltd., Langley Brothers and W. Walker Ltd.

Mr. Seddon expressed appreciation of the close liaison of the Stoke-on-Trent City Council and the building employers, of which the scheme was a prime example.

With the local building industry suffering acutely from a shortage of work, and large numbers of their labour force having to travel considerable distances to find work, the need for liaison had never been closer.

Bucknall Flats nearing completion.

The New Central Library in Hanley was officially opened on Thursday, December 10th, 1970 by The Right Honourable Baroness Jennie Lee of Asheridge, wife of Aneurin (Nye) Bevan, who established the National Health Service. She unveiled a commemorative plaque at the entrance of this high-profile building. An 11 page brochure – describing the new facility as 'traditional and conventional' - was developed for the opening event, which carried pictures of various rooms throughout the building and gave facts and figures such as the book shelf capacity – overall some 257,000 books, 2,300 maps and 35,000 documents.

This brochure gave an overview of the building's structure and fit-out in considerable detail, describing it as being *'of reinforced concrete and the whole sub-divided into three separate but continuous blocks with a bridged gap between to minimise the possible effects of mining subsidence. It is centrally heated from a separate solid fuel installation, also serving the Police headquarters by means of water coils embedded within the structural floor slabs at each level.*

Wall finishes include paint, wallpaper, Laconite ply boarding, polished fossil limestone slabs, simulated leather, acoustic tile and natural timbers. The building is fitted with vertical fitted louvre blinds. Seddon (Stoke) Ltd are the general contractors at the tender price of £433,615.'

Signing the contracts for the construction of a new factory for the ribbon manufacturers Berisfords, at Congleton.

A Catholic Exhibition took place at Burslem Town Hall in 1960, and Seddon was charged with supplying, fixing and dismantling the frame and surface materials at the event on behalf of Wood, Goldstraw and Yorath.

Building homes in the Silkmore Lane area of Stafford in 1964.
Picture courtesy of Bill Rockey

Bill Rockey, pictured in 1968. Bill started with the company in 1961 as a labourer and went on to work for more than 30 years with Seddon. He was well-regarded as a highly competent driver and operator of plant vehicles, able to cope with the most demanding of jobs. However, in 1968 he blotted his copybook after tipping over a jib on a crane at a building site in Burslem. Workmen darted for cover as the cab toppled, but no-one was injured and Bill carried on for another 20 years doing the same job without incident.

Picture courtesy of Bill Rockey

Some of the Seddon team from around the late 1960s on a construction site, believed to be Edensor School in Stoke-on-Trent. Included on the picture are Bill Rockey and Joe Pawel, both in white shirts.

Picture courtesy of Bill Rockey

The opening of the M6 through Staffordshire created new business opportunities for Seddon. This picture shows the new motorway – with no crash barrier – in the area around Seabridge, in Newcastle-under-Lyme.

Picture courtesy of The Potteries Museum and Art Gallery

HALL EXTENSIONS BRING THEATRE TO SUBURBS

New £9,000 extensions to the Harold Clowes Community Hall, Bentilee, designed to bring theatre to the suburbs, were officially opened last night.

And after the opening by the Lord Mayor, Alderman James Evans, the new stage which has been provided by the Community Association was "baptised" with a drama production by the New Intimate Theatre Company.

Performing the opening ceremony the Lord Mayor likened the city's community halls to the village and church halls which provided for the recreation of scattered communities.

He went on: "We still require such places because the community centre provides a vital need in this material age.

"With the continuous movement of people there is a danger of losing our most precious assets of friendliness and good neighbourliness."

Since the last war, the Lord Mayor said, the city council had been engaged in vast slum clearance schemes and the rehousing of people in new estates, where the old time neighbourly spirit was not as much in evidence as it used to be.

"Wonderful"

"These community halls," he said, "provide wonderful opportunities for people to get together and get to know each other."

The Harold Clowes Community Hall, he recalled, was built in 1956 and several extensions had culminated in the fifth and final stage.

The Lord Mayor was introduced by the Chairman of the Extension Committee, Mr. E. Seddon, who said the full cost of the building was now in the region of £50,000.

In a vote of thanks to the Lord Mayor, the Community Association President, Sir Harold Clowes, recalled that it was in 1954 that he was approached by a group of builders who wished to mark his period as Chairman of the Housing Committee.

At first the builders had talked of providing some other form of building but he had persuaded them otherwise and the Harold Clowes Community Hall was the result.

He went on: "We believe facilities for leisure are [illegible]

At the official opening of the new stage extension at the Harold Clowes Community Centre last night the Chairman, Sir Harold Clowes, is seen presenting inscribed plaques to Mr. Ernest Seddon, Chairman of the Extension Committee, Mr. Harry Taylor, Mr. Harry Hand, Mr. Ernest Simpson and Mr. Bill Leake. To the left are the Town Clerk, Mr. L. Keith Robinson, and the Lord Mayor, Alderman J. Evans, who officially opened the extensions.

'CITY'S POST-AN EXAMPLE'

Opening of Clowes Hall on Ubberley Estate

Ministry Secretary's Praise

Stoke-on-Trent's post-war housing record was yesterday held up as an example to local authorities in other parts of the country, by Dame Evelyn Sharp, Permanent Secretary to the Ministry of Housing and Local Government.

She was speaking at Fenton Town Hall after the opening of the Harold Clowes Community Hall on the Ubberley Farm housing estate. The Hall had been presented to the city by the 43 builders and 35 building materials suppliers, who have been engaged on council house building in Stoke-on-Trent, in recognition of the services to city housing of Mr. Clowes, who was Chairman of the City Housing Committee from 1950 to 1955.

Dame Evelyn said such a gift was unique in her experience of local government. She praised the co-operation which existed between builders in the city and the local authority and the extraordinary feat of organisation by the Council and Mr. Clowes which enabled the builders to carry out their work.

In building more than 12,000 houses since the war, Stoke-on-Trent had achieved a splendid record for an authority of its size.

Fine Example

In gaining the housing medal with its exhibition of improvements made to modernise older-type houses, the city had set a fine example to the whole country she said.

Though the city's record was good compared with other local authorities, however, there were still thousands more houses which could be improved with the help of grants.

"It is a source of disappointment and puzzlement to my Minister that more is not being done with the generous grants available for modernising older houses," she said.

At the opening ceremony Mr. E. Seddon, Chairman of the Hall Erection Committee, referred to the exemplary leadership of Mr. Clowes as Chairman of the Housing Committee.

The Hall was dedicated by the Rev. A. Perry " in thanksgiving for the work of Harold Clowes."

Thanking the donors, the Lord Mayor, Mr. H. Naylor, who was accompanied by the Lady Mayoress and the Deputy Lord Mayor (Alder-

spoke of the team spirit which existed between builders suppliers and the Corporation, and described the gift of the hall as "a magnificent, public-spirited gesture."

Schools Programme

Speaking at the Jubilee Hall, Stoke, in the evening, at a dinner organised by the North Staffordshire Building Trades Employers' Association, the Lord Mayor dealt with the future building programme and referred to five new schools proposed in the Bentilee and Berryhill areas.

He said a new school at Bentilee costing about £120,000 was in the 1956-57 programme. At Berryhill in the same year there was a proposed infants' county secondary school to cost about £62,000, and a junior school to cost about £70,000 the following year.

In the same area, it was proposed in 1957-58 to build a further infants' school at a cost of about £60,000 and a further junior school to cost about £70,000.

At about the same time, subject to Ministry permission, it was also proposed to build a county secondary modern school in the same area at a cost of about £200,000.

The Lord Mayor pointed out that, in addition to the vast housing programme, 35 new schools had been built in the city since the war; there were four first-class homes for the aged; home help and home nursing services were being developed; a department for the physically handicapped was beginning to take shape; and a social club for the blind was to be established.

The City Council planned to cater for the needy, the sick and the afflicted, he said, and though this might be expen-

A spirit of co-operation prevailed in the 1950s and 1960s - and a feeling that builders across the region played a positive role in the city of Stoke-on-Trent moving out of the doldrums and into a brighter future. This is best reflected in these two newspaper articles from The Sentinel. The first, dated 1956, describes how all builders involved in the post war building programme had joined forces to present Sir Harold Clowes, a leading light in the construction of the city in his capacity as Chairman of the City's Housing Committee, with the Harold Clowes Centre, for the community of Bentilee. The second article, from 1962, reports on the opening of a new extension to the hall and reflects on the co-operation between homebuilders that enabled slum clearance programmes to take place and 12,000 new properties to be built after the war – a considerable feat. Both articles quote Ernest Seddon.

Newspaper cuttings courtesy of The Sentinel

A.C.E. HOISTS

Construction News

FIELDING & BACON
Bilton Road Erith
tel Erith 40711

the formwork people

No. 5265   THURSDAY, AUGUST 17, 1972   10p

Unions hold line against all-out stoppage

BIG SHUTDOWN BEGINS

'Threat from the Heavy Gang'

IN YORKSHIRE there have been allegations of violence which could result in the Yorkshire Federation of Building Trade Employers sending a report to the Home Office.

Trouble started last Thursday at the Crossley Terrace local authority housing development in Halifax.

Peter Fee, director of J. and J. Fee, told CN: "I arrived at the site last week to find 20 men at the entrance. They in no way at tempted to impede my entry, but there were another 100 men swarming all over the site.

"They had turned off compressors and mixers and thoroughly scared the workmen on the site. An official showed me his credentials and asked if he could address my men at the canteen.

"During the course of the meeting my men were threatened with the heavy gang from Leeds.

"Throughout the whole of the meeting men outside the site were throwing stones and bricks at the canteen," declared Mr Fee.

"Very few men will stand up to that sort of abuse. On Monday another gang of about 20 men returned to the site and made a house to house search for men working.

"Most of the men who were working left, but the 'flying pickets' said they would return each day to check that the site had stopped completely.

Colin Hogan, Yorkshire regional director of the NFBTE told CN: "There is a mobile militant minority who have been moving around the Yorkshire region by bus and car these ening and intimidating operations.

"I shall be recommending to members that they report to officers of their kind to the police.

"We are collating all the information and I hope we shall be able to send a full report to the Home Secretary."

Len McLay, TGWU regional secretary in Leeds, told CN "Allegations of this nature made by the employers are totally without foundation. Small incidents are being magnified out of all proportion.

"There have been reports of violence which I have checked out with the police. Far from condemning the pickets the police have complimented them on their behaviour.

"These lads are very well organised and I am entirely happy that everything is under control."

THIS WEEK

Box girder tests ...	3
Contracts ...	8
People ...	10
Plant news ... 12, 13, 14,	15
Planning ...	18
Regional news 19, 20, 21,	22
600 cu m of concrete laid in a day ...	24

The top leadership of the construction trade unions this week declared themselves against an uncontrolled spread of militant action which is threatening a massive shutdown of the industry.

Recognising the decisions already made by the regions to escalate the dispute, they are asking the action committees which confer again in London today to intensify the campaign but to stick to the concerted policy of disciplined action.

But there is to be an important shift in tactics. The squeeze is now to be put on the smaller regional contractors who, the unions think, will be an easier target than the powerful national contracting firms who have held steady in the face of intensive action.

Many of the big sites have been closed for weeks but no company has so far deviated from the National Federation policy of standing by firms under attack. Now the unions are to pick on firms employing from 60 to 200 workers.

Reviewing the confused situation which developed after the rumour spread that the unions were about to do a deal with the employers, it is understood that the top leadership now regard this as demonstrating the fact that they cannot take the membership any faster than they will go.

They were willing to try for a settlement but the subsequent rumpus showed that the majority would not have it.

The meeting of the NJC operatives' side on Tuesday is said to have taken place in a calm and reflective atmosphere, no doubt induced by the magnitude of the issues facing the union leadership and the heavy costs of a prolonged stoppage.

It is also understood that though their policy is to give full support to members acting in accordance with union instructions, TGWU are considering withdrawal of strike pay in line with UCATT.

The atmosphere on Tuesday was not assisted by the advertisements which the building trades employers inserted in the national press on the morning of the meeting.

These accused the union leadership of going back on recognisance of what the employers described as the "best and biggest offer ever made in the industry's history."

This, according to the employers, was due to the action of extremists determined to keep the dispute going.

This was hotly denied by the trade union side. Len Eason, London regional secretary of UCATT and well known for his moderate views, told CN that his members took their decision to shut down central London at a crowded meeting which was certainly not packed with extremists.

"When we put it to the vote," said Mr Eaton, "the decision was unanimous. I have never seen such a solid vote. Every hand went up.

"Why was the reaction so strong? Well, our people are fed up, not only over the wages offer, but also because of the corruption of self employment, the vagaries of pseudo bonus schemes, and the heavy reliance on overtime to get a decent wage packet.

"The men in London are ready for a long fight if this is the only way to clean up the building industry."

Mr Eaton said that over the next two weeks they would try to close every building site within an area as far north of the Thames as Swiss Cottage and Hackney and as far south as Battersea Park. This is being enforced by full time officials assisted by the walking pickets.

In Birmingham a widening circle of sites is being closed by means of strike notices served by secretaries of the trade unions. Similar action is being taken in the north west and most other regions.

In Scotland, union officials worked hard to persuade men to return to the "disciplined escalation" policy after some 15,000 came out in unofficial protest against acceptance of the bonus offer.

In the rest of Scotland many sites returned to work but B. W. Campbell, director of the Scottish NFBTE, said that they were heavily restricted in output by the withdrawal of bonus and the ban on overtime.

Mr Campbell said he was convinced that what the unions were calling "spontaneous demonstration" was carefully engineered by militants.

"It seems to have been a well planned operation," said Mr Campbell. "And indicates the work of a fairly well organised group of activists outside the trade union movement."

Union sources reported that three firms in Hull and one in Leeds were on the point of signing agreements which would concede the £25 basic rates plus £5 guaranteed bonus, but no confirmation of these reports could be obtained before CN went to press.

Macmillan watches but stays clear

MR HEATH and government ministers regard the pay demands of Britain's striking building workers as "highly inflationary".

And Maurice Macmillan the employment secretary is not prepared to step in with his department's conciliation carrier unless severe hardship is threatened to the community, or one side or the other in the dispute requests his intervention.

This was stated in Whitehall as Mr Macmillan, already chained to his desk by the dock dispute, kept a "close watch" on the building strike situation.

As CN went to press, ministers insisted that the dispute was still caught up in "normal industrial machinery and they were "keeping an eye on the situation".

But no approach had been made to the Employment Department to conciliate. The ministry would step in if:

EITHER the employers or the unions made an approach to Mr Macmillan on which came the other side would also be called in.

THE situation was so disastrous that the well being of the community was being affected. In this situation Mr Macmillan would ask for a situation report.

Neither of these stages had been reached and the department was "fairly open minded".

But ministers noted that the unions are talking about "big guns" — the employers have offered a 14 per cent deal but the unions are demanding £30 for a 35 hour week.

Marples Ridgway for M56 in Cheshire?

CN understands that Marples-Ridgway, Bath, are well placed for the award of the £6.3 million contract no. 7 which forms the central section of the M56.

The contract is for 10.25 km from Preston brook to the start of the M6, at a point just south of its existing interchange with the A56 at Lymm, and will be concurrent with contract no. 8, due to be awarded shortly.

Construction will include the dual, three lane carriageways, 13 bridges, a two-level interchange at Stretton and a new graded interchange at Lymm.

Design and supervision of the contract is by the Cheshire sub-unit of the North Western Road Construction Unit.

Carlisle underpass

Border Engineering, Whitehaven are believed to be well placed for award of the £700,000 contract for the underpass section of the Carlisle bypass.

Chapter 4 Strikes and Shortages

Seddon In The 1970s And 1980s

The long, hot summer of 1976 saw temperatures sizzle – but the nation's outlook was not always sunny. Britain in the 70s was dogged by problems, including high inflation, high taxes, strikes - and the famous Winter of Discontent.

A scene from the Winter of Discontent.
Picture – Getty Images

Although the mood nationally was often stuck in the doldrums, at Seddon the workers enjoyed a relatively stable work environment, as management steered the company on a steady course. The company minutes show there was plenty of work in the early 1970s, although labour shortages were an issue.

The National Building Strike in the early 1970s saw British construction brought to its knees. Strikes in the early seventies rocked the construction industry, with scenes like this, pictured below, a common sight across the UK.

Picket lines could become aggressive flashpoints, as strikers battled to stop others in the industry trying to cross the line to get to work. Many Seddon workers wanted to carry on as usual, and the company used private cars to get their men on site – vans with company names or other trade identification would be stopped on the picket line, but men in plain cars were usually allowed to go on.

Picketing of construction sites was common during the early 1970s.
Picture – Getty Images

Generally for Seddon staff, the mood was calm, but a difficult situation developed as painters from Seddon broke the picket line to get work moving at the City General Hospital in Stoke-on-Trent. John Hallam **(pictured above)**, a foreman painter at Seddon, remembers some pickets getting hold of the painters in the hospital and lining them up – threatening violence with baseball bats. A senior nurse heard the commotion and went to investigate. Quickly aware of what was happening, she turned to one of the strikers – the largest and most vocal of the group - and calmly said: 'I'm looking at you, and I'm remembering your face, and hoping you never have to come into this hospital. Let these men get on with their work – this ward is needed.' Her words worked and the group dispersed.

Under the union rules, apprentices did not strike and a young Cyril Wakefield found himself with one other apprentice working on the Wedgwood Farm site, near Chell, where private homes had been built, but work had, in the main, stopped with the strike. John Seddon would periodically check on the youngsters to see they were safe and well. The experience did not have a detrimental effect on Cyril – he went on to buy his first home on the Wedgwood Estate, and became a senior member of staff within the Seddon Building company.

Cyril's new home, purchased for £7,500 came complete with the specification for a turquoise bathroom suite. The vogue for coloured bathroom suites was a key feature of 1970s interior design trends **(see opposite)**. However, Cyril's colour choice was an unusual one. 'Avocado' was the most popular choice and Seddon found that potential homeowners would insist on this for their house – sometimes refusing to purchase a property unless they were sure it came with the colour scheme in place.

Cyril Wakefield pictured in the 1970s.

These three pictures reflect the vogue for coloured bathrooms. Colours such as avocado and sepia represented the height of fashion, although this colour chart shows that many more colours were available for the modern bathroom.

All pictures courtesy of Twyfords

Colour range This page shows the range of available colours.

Every effort has been made to ensure accurate colour reproduction, minor variations may occur in the printing process, making it impossible to guarantee an exact match with the ceramic glaze.

Twyfords colours are matched by leading bath manufacturers.

TWYFORDS

Twyfords Bathrooms
PO Box 23 Stoke-on-Trent ST4 7AL England
Telephone 0782 29531   Telex 36282

Almond	Alpine	Avocado	Cameo	Harlequin Avocado	Harlequin Pampas

Damask	Mink	Pampas	Sandalwood	Sepia	Harlequin Sandalwood

2.1

Inflation Takes Its Toll

Purchasing a home in Wedgwood Farm, and other properties across Britain, was not a straightforward affair in the 1970s. Inflation and economic controls made home-ownership an uphill task. In order to control the supply of money, The Bank of England would only allow building societies to lend a certain amount. In general, building societies were not able to lend money for a mortgage unless the person requesting the money was a member of the society and had been saving for a number of years.

There was a desire to buy property, but many found it impossible to fulfil their dream of home ownership. Seddon actually closed off Wedgwood Farm for two years because, although people were clambering to buy the properties, they had no way of securing a mortgage. The homes sold later when money supply controls were eventually lifted.

Inflation was under the spotlight in 1972, when Ernest Seddon reported to the Board of Directors, that *'short term, he felt very concerned about the inflationary process going on but, over a longer period of time, felt the English character would impose itself on the troubles and we would get back to a more sensible way of living.'*

However, the problem was not to go away so soon. 1973 marked one of the most significant economic crises of this era – when OPEC (Organisation of the Petroleum Exporting Companies) decided to double the price of oil – causing inflation to rocket further.

Alan Liddell, a Regional Director of the Seddon Painting company, has records which show that in one year in the 1970s wages rose from 7s 11d in January, 8s 9d in Feb – to 9s 3d in November, due to inflation. As a result, in 1974, the Directors decided not to tender for any fixed price contracts unless they were short-term projects.

Even later into the decade, pricing was difficult to predict. A £15,000 order for copper piping had to be placed months in advance to guarantee delivery, but in the three months between December 1978 when the order had been placed and February 1979 – when Seddon were awaiting delivery - the price increased an incredible 12 times, to an overall growth of 19 per cent on the original price.

International issues also had an effect on Seddon. Idi Amin, the African dictator **(pictured opposite)**, forced thousands of Asians from Uganda in the 1970s, and many came to the UK to rebuild their lives. Seddon builders and painters were drafted in to prepare Raleigh Hall, Drake Hall and Loggerheads Hospital - all situated on the Staffordshire border with Shropshire - to house the refugees. The team worked around the clock, even carrying out what is known in the industry as 'ghosting' –

literally working day and night over a fixed time period – to get the work done.

Trouble closer to home beckoned in the North West, when painters were also drafted in to refurbish Chester's tax office, which was damaged by a bomb planted by Welsh Nationalists. The blast occurred in 1969, and Seddon were on site in the 1970s to paint the refurbished building.

Although work continued in the North West and North Wales, in 1971 Seddon closed its office in Anglesey, due to a shortage of work and the yard and office were put on the market for £7,500.

Longton Hall

A major project in the 1970s for Seddon was the construction of another housing estate, off Longton Hall Road in Blurton, which had started off in the 1960s, as mentioned in Chapter Three. In the 1950s, Blurton had

been the centre for construction of three-storey flats in Tollgate Court, as well as council properties in and around Beaconsfield Drive, and neighbouring Newstead. High-rise flats, as shown on page 51, were also constructed in the area.

By contrast, one of the features of the Longton Hall development was the large number of bungalows. Modern demands on space have rendered the building of single storey homes uneconomical and the construction of bungalows on a large scale is now rarely seen. Despite the attraction of single-storey living, the project also included another set of flats, this time on land behind St Paul's Church in Longton Hall Road. A number of these properties are still owned by Seddon Estates.

St Paul's Church and Seddon came together to mark the life of one of the company's loyal employees, Ken Sproston. Ken had been a warden at St Paul's and, upon his death in 1979, his work friends built a memorial wall

Idi Amin, the African dictator. Seddon helped refurbish properties in the Midlands to house those fleeing his leadership in 1970s Uganda.

Picture – Getty Images

This entrance replaces
a memorial garden to
KENNETH SPROSTON
(1915–1979)

The Three Day Week

Many remember Britain in the 1970s for the dire effects of the three-day working week. Introduced to conserve energy, as coal supplies to power stations were reduced, industry was severely affected.

For those working on outdoor sites, such as new school programmes, the three-day week did not take such a toll, with diesel generators able to deliver the power needed. However, on indoor sites, such as factories, the lights would go out and time had to be called on work until power was resumed.

in the grounds of the church. Years later, the wall had to be removed for extension work, but this memorial plaque **(pictured above)**, is situated within the building as a lasting reminder of his life.

Longton Hall had been home to one of the first pottery companies to set up in the city, back in the 1700s, and work on site had to stop for some time as archaeologists identified various historical treasures in the ground during the construction process.

The estate went on to develop a literary theme – the roads at Longton Hall were named after poets, with names such as Tennyson and Browning.

Seddon carried out a major project valued at around £1 million to build a new factory for Shires in Longton, which was completed in 1976. Shires was affected by the energy shortage, and that had a knock-on effect on the work in progress, but the job was completed and Seddon were praised by company representatives at the official opening.

This aerial shot shows St Paul's Church years before Seddon started building work. Longton Hall Farm is pictured to the right of the church.
Photograph courtesy of St Paul's Church.

Work in action on site at Shires.
Pictures courtesy of
Cyril Wakefield

A Change In Leadership

Ernest Seddon handed over the reins to his son John in 1974, when he stood down as Chairman. His son also continued as Managing Director. In turn, John's son, Stuart – who had entered the trade in 1978 as a bricklayer – attended his first Board meeting in 1983.

The early 1970s brought other changes in leadership within the company. June 1973 marked the retirement of Arnold Hadley, who had been one of the major pillars of the Seddon company. Such was Arnold's close involvement with the firm that John Seddon senior, co-founder of the company, looked upon him as one of his sons. Arnold was made a Director of G & J Seddon in 1946, heading up the Surveying department. He played a major part in the development of Seddon (Stoke) Limited and was responsible for the company's surveyors working out of The Potteries. Gordon Fishwick then headed the department and Cyril Adams was later appointed as the Director in 1963. Arnold's retirement party took place at the Midland Hotel in Manchester and, as a gift from the Directors, he received a Triumph Stag sports car.

Cyril Adams had joined the company from school, as a trainee Quantity Surveyor and went on within the company to lead this vital part of the business operations for more than 30 years. He was highly-admired across the whole industry for his professionalism and leadership.

In 1972, another appointment was made to the Board, with Terry Smith taking up a senior role in the company. Terry served his apprenticeship as a joiner with Seddon, and then went on to work as a Contracts Manager, working on private housing sites across Stoke-on-Trent. The experience and insight gained on these projects put him in good stead for the rest of his working life with the company. He opened a regional office in Congleton in the early 1970s and from there oversaw hundreds of contracts – including school construction work – for Cheshire County Council.

In 1975 another appointment was made to the Board, when Peter Mottram – who joined Seddon as a trainee surveyor – was made a Director of Seddon (Stoke).

Arnold Hadley and his wife at his retirement party at the Midland Hotel in Manchester.

66

John Seddon became Chairman of Seddon Group in 1978 and he insisted Andrew Brown **(pictured overleaf)** became Company Secretary of the Group to work alongside him. Andrew had previously been Company Secretary of Seddon (Stoke) and a Director of Seddon Properties. For 40 years, Andrew worked for Seddon, starting out on-site under Percy Woolridge and Jack Finney, after completing National Service in the RAF and a university degree. Andrew was the driving force in developing many housing sites including Longton Hall Farm and Wedgwood Farm. He died in 2006, aged 75.

Peter Mottram, who joined Seddon as a Trainee Surveyor, was appointed a Director of the company in 1975.

Technological Breakthroughs

Innovations in construction equipment continued to develop, with a particular emphasis on hand-held power tools.

For certain pieces of equipment, training was required to ensure the work was carried out safely. One tool that Seddon used in the 1970s - an explosive nail-gun - needed to be handled with particular caution.

Resembling a hand-held pistol, the gun was powered by a cartridge, which would blast nails into walls. On one occasion, at a new-build project, the gun was accidentally

set off in a toilet cubicle and the nails flew through 10 cubicle walls in total. This type of nail-gun was quickly abandoned by Seddon, due to the dangerous power it delivered.

Away from the building site, in the Seddon office, hand-operated large accounting machines, known as the Burroughs L5000, were well-used in the 1970s. Minutes show these were replaced by a new, more advanced electronic version L9500 in 1976 – but their days were numbered. In 1981, Seddon purchased three IBM computers for £59,000, one for Seddon (Stoke), one for G & J Seddon and one for Seddons (Plant and Engineers) - to replace the Burroughs machines, and the company marked its start into the exciting new computing era.

Although computers now dominate the Stoke headquarters of Seddon, and regional offices, Sheila Dobson still prefers to use her Burroughs L9500 machine for complex calculations. She joined the company in 1970 and more than 30 years later has remained loyal to this type of machine.

Andrew Brown is pictured at the top left of the table at a Seddon Group AGM in 1995. Around the table in a clockwise direction are John Seddon at the head of the table, David Seddon, Ian Pinnington, Christopher Seddon, George Seddon and Patricia Potter.

Another now commonplace piece of equipment which came into use in the 1970s and 1980s was the mobile phone. This went on to revolutionise the industry, with painters and builders able to travel further afield, without struggling to contact the office. Early use was a challenge in itself however. The phones were cumbersome pieces of kit, with massive battery packs.

Prior to having a mobile phone, John Seddon had an in-car system set up by the Automobile Association (AA) whereby he could call their headquarters with the codename White Whisky Two, and get them to deliver a message via the landline to selected recipients. Walkie talkies were also a popular means of communication on-site, before mobile phones took off.

Another development at this time was the advent of metrification. Bricks were affected by the change from Imperial to Metric in the 1970s - and a new size metric

brick was used to replace the traditional nine inch brick. Expert brick-layers, including Graham Smith, **(pictured below),** and Lou Norris, worked hard to introduce the new 30 centimetre bricks, which were used on projects including the Harrison Mayer factory in Stoke-on-Trent and Fallibroome High School in Macclesfield – but their use was short-lived. Brick manufacturers eventually went back to the original size brick, but measured in the metric size of 225 millimetres.

At Fallibroome High School in Macclesfield, Cheshire, bricks were a never-ending sight for Seddon employee Joe Pawel (known to many fondly as Joe the Pole). He had to cut 22,000 of the new metric bricks by hand at the site, as part of the building work to follow the structure's roofline. He tackled the job with humour and determination - and when it rained the men on site built a canopy over him for protection.

Across the rest of Cheshire, the county became a major source of work for Seddon, as it built new schools under serial contracts, introduced by the then Education Minister, Margaret Thatcher. Many people were involved in these projects, including Terry Smith who was the Contract Director based in the area office at Congleton.

Graham Smith

Fallibroome High School, pictured above, in Cheshire, built using metric bricks. Liz Wilson from the school is pictured below, comparing a modern brick with the short-lived early metric version.

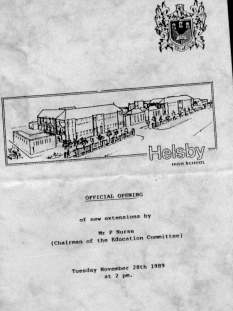

Helsby
HIGH SCHOOL

OFFICIAL OPENING

of new extensions by

Mr P Nurse
(Chairman of the Education Committee)

Tuesday November 28th 1989
at 2 pm.

The front page of a booklet for the official opening of Helsby High School, built by Seddon.

Congleton Borough Council
Housing Department
BRUNSWICK STREET HOUSING DEVELOPMENT
CONGLETON

The Official Opening by
His Worship The Mayor,
Councillor E. C. Gill, B.Sc.,
Wednesday, 14th April, 1976

George Allen at Sale Car Park.
Pictures and information courtesy of George Allen

Brunswick Street Flats in Congleton.

Other work in the county included Brunswick Street Flats, in Congleton, and Sale Multi-Storey Car Park.

A Fear Of Crime

A cult television programme during the 1970s was The Sweeney, the drama about the workings of Scotland Yard's Flying Squad - tackling armed robberies and other violent crimes in and around London, all in a day's work.

However, armed robberies were not just a concern in the Capital city. At Seddon, with hundreds of builders and painters paid in cash, the amount of money handled on pay day was massive – and presented a real safety risk.

During the 1970s, ways of coping with security were a predominant subject, appearing throughout the company's minutes. In fact, the minutes for the 10th September 1971 report that some men in a car with false plates had been taking pictures of the office – an activity that raised a great deal of suspicion.

At one stage Seddon were told by the Flying Squad that they had received intelligence the company was being targeted for a robbery by a south-east based criminal gang. The police had established when and where the robbery was set to take place and took the necessary action to prevent the crime being committed.

A scene from the TV series The Sweeney.
Picture copyright of FremantleMedia

Seddon's insurance company put in place strict guidelines for the transportation of cash from the bank to Duke Street – where wages were paid from an armoured, reinforced cash office in the transport department – including the stipulation that two cars made the cash-collection journey, each with a driver and escort.

In 1980, Seddon set up an incentive scheme to encourage people to have their wages paid directly into the bank – with a £50 weekly prize draw organised for those participating. The first name to be drawn for the cash prize was Stuart Seddon – but his father insisted the draw was made again.

The Cold War Bites

Fears of a Soviet attack on UK shores dominated television, radio and print throughout the 1970s and early 1980s. People lived in fear of nuclear war and some people even acted on their concerns and built nuclear bunkers in their gardens.

Seddon were involved in a major project around 1982 to create a secret nuclear bunker – in the heart of Cheshire.

Originally built in the 1950s, Hack Green had been used as a top-secret radar station. However, in the 1980s, it

was converted to fit another secret role - as a nuclear bunker from where Cold War operations could be carried out.

As part of the refurbishment project, the team at Seddon used ultra-high powered water jets to cut through three feet wide concrete walls.

The site – called Hack Green Secret Nuclear Bunker - is now a tourist attraction.

Another feature of this time was the build-up of RAF bases on the Eastern side of the country, put in place to deliver a fast response to any Communist Block threat to the UK.

They generated a large amount of work and, as a result, York's painting office went from strength to strength, carrying out projects at major sites for the Ministry of Defence along the North East coast and inland. York office, at this time, was under the control of Bill Gibson, who went on to become a Divisional Director within Seddon.

One massive project was the Army's Catterick Garrison, situated off the A1 in Yorkshire, which ran for a number of years in the early 1970s. Such was the size of the job that at one time there were 300 Seddon staff on site including up to 50 apprentices.

New company offices were starting to open across the country, but there was still a fair amount of lodging for workers. On several occasions, workmen found they had

The Hack Green Secret Nuclear Bunker
Picture courtesy of Robert Siebert, the curator of Hack Green Secret Nuclear Bunker.

to share rooms with a number of their colleagues after the landlord or landlady decided to make financial gains and cram them in. Harry Richards once found he had to share a room with six others at a guest house in Anglesey. However, this started to change as new centres were created away from the company's Stoke-on-Trent heartlands and the workforce became much more local to the area in which they worked. Before the Cheltenham office opened in the 1980s for painters, Darren Bowkett, (**pictured above**), who joined the company as a YTS apprentice, remembers working out of a van across the region.

Into the 1980s

The troubles of the 1970s continued into the next decade – where lean times dominated working patterns in the early years. The 1980s were characterised by a lot of smaller sized jobs – and a good deal of travelling around the country to reach them. This process was to form the basis of the company's move in later years as a national

contractor, developing offices and premises at major sites across the UK.

In time, improved road links, a more geographically diverse work load and the advent of mobile communications would all help the company branch out from the Potteries to open many more regional offices.

UK expansion was on the cards, but the introduction into the new decade was not a good one. In 1980, a Government moratorium led to a massive cut in labour, particularly for painters. Work was brought to a halt almost immediately and walls were left unpainted as workers were forced to leave sites.

For Seddon, the blue sky on the horizon came from Tytherington, in Cheshire, situated on the outskirts of Macclesfield, where a large-scale construction programme dominated the workload for the company in this period. A spectacular club house was also built at the golf course by G & J Seddon.

Most of the homes on the Tytherington site were built by Seddon (Stoke), totalling approximately 500 properties.

First bricks being laid on the site at Tytherington in 1982 with the ruin of Tytherington Old Hall in the background. This building, which dates back to the 1700s, was fully restored by Seddon and later became Group headquarters until 2004.

Mrs. Traudi Plesch, chairman of the pool fund, being presented with the cheque for £2,007, by Mr. Harry Richards (right). Also seen are headmistress Mrs. Vicky Christmas and Mr. Cyril Adams, a director of Seddons.

Charity walkers aid pool appeal

A big-hearted building firm working on a therapeutic pool at Wolstanton have gone a step further to help its completion.

Thirty-five employees of Seddons (Stoke) Ltd. took part in a 10 mile sponsored walk and, with the help of donations, have raised more than £2,000 towards the bill for the project at Merryfields Special School.

And yesterday a cheque was presented to the chairman of the appeal fund Mrs. Traudi Plesch by walk organiser, quantity surveyor Mr. Harry Richards.

It brings the total amount raised to date up to £89,000. The ultimate target is £104,000.

"The cheque includes more than 500 donations from friends and colleagues of Seddons and I would like to thank them for their help,"

said Mr. Richards.

The pool will be used for special exercises for the handicapped children at the school in Boon-avenue.

Building work has been temporarily halted during the freezing weather conditions which have put the project slightly behind schedule. The pool is expected to be completed by June.

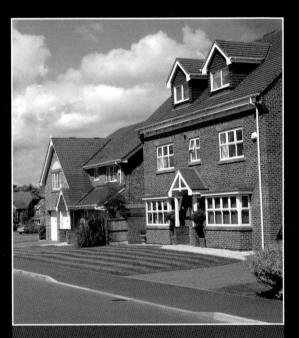

Homes built at Tytherington by Seddon. Although work started in the 1980s the company has continued to build prestigious homes into the new Millennium at the Cheshire site, with work more recently carried out by Seddon Homes, part of the Seddon Group.

A newspaper cutting about a therapeutic hydrotherapy centre, built by Seddon at Merryfields School, a centre for special needs youngsters, in Newcastle-under-Lyme. A major fund-raising scheme was launched to help pay for the centre, and Seddon staff contributed with a sponsored walk. At the opening, the youngsters performed a play to show their new facility, and went on stage wearing Seddon hard hats and high visibility vests.

Painting a hospital at Teeside in 1980.
Picture courtesy of Ken Starr.

British Troops Land On the Falklands.
The conflict over the Falkland Islands dominated the news in the 1980s and had a far-reaching effect across the UK. As war broke out, Seddon were awaiting the delivery of a £7,500 printer - ordered from Argentina. This was delayed and an alternative had to be arranged. Picture – Getty Images

A job well done. Some of the team who built a Catholic High School in Newcastle-under-Lyme.
Picture courtesy of Peter Clarke, who was General Foreman on the project.

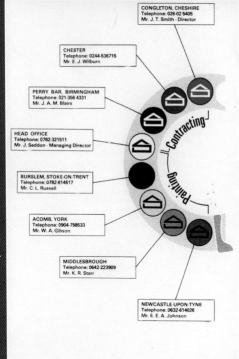

CONGLETON, CHESHIRE
Telephone: 026-02 5405
Mr. J. T. Smith - Director

CHESTER
Telephone: 0244-536715
Mr. E. J. Wilburn

PERRY BAR, BIRMINGHAM
Telephone: 021-356 4331
Mr. J. A. M. Blairs

HEAD OFFICE
Telephone: 0782-321511
Mr. J. Seddon - Managing Director

BURSLEM, STOKE-ON-TRENT
Telephone: 0782-814617
Mr. C. L. Russell

ACOMB, YORK
Telephone: 0904-798533
Mr. W. A. Gibson

MIDDLESBROUGH
Telephone: 0642-223909
Mr. K. R. Starr

NEWCASTLE-UPON-TYNE
Telephone: 0632-614026
Mr. E. E. A. Johnson

Contracting
Painting

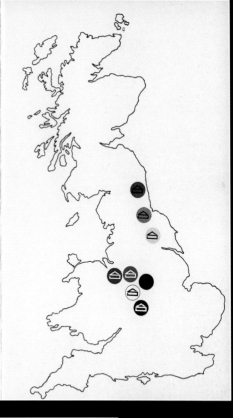

ILLUSTRATIONS

1. Fallibroome High School, Priory Lane, Macclesfield.
2. Industrial Development in Stoke-on-Trent.
3. Private Housing Development for Seddon Estates Ltd. in Chelford, Cheshire.

SEDDON (STOKE) LIMITED
Brief Company History

In 1897 George and John Seddon set up business in Little Hulton, near Worsley, Manchester. The partnership thrived and in 1921 a limited company was formed as G. & J. Seddon Ltd.

The business continued to thrive and expand. In 1932 G. & J. Seddon Ltd. started working in Stoke-on-Trent and continued working as a branch office of G. & J. Seddon Ltd. until 1957.

In 1957 G. & J. Seddon Ltd. was re-organised into the form that it is today, and Seddon (Stoke) Ltd. was created as a separate limited company.

It is, therefore, 25 years since Seddon (Stoke) Ltd. was registered, although 50 years since Seddons started working in Stoke-on-Trent.

The Directors of Seddon (Stoke) Ltd. are:-

Mr. J. Seddon	— Managing Director
Mr. C. K. Adams	— Q.S. Director
Mr. J. T. Smith	— Contracts Director
Mr. P. M. H. Mottram	— Painting Director
Mr. B. J. Mellor	— Company Secretary

The Company is well known as Building, Painting and Public Works Contractors and has for over 40 years played a major role in the day to day maintenance of Public Buildings and Services.

Subsequently branch offices have been established, in addition to Head Office in Fenton, Stoke-on-Trent, both for building and painting contracts. Building Contracting branch offices in Congleton, Birmingham and Chester, and Painting branch offices in Burslem, York, Newcastle-upon-Tyne and Middlesbrough.

Design and estimating facilities are centralised at Head Office, while each branch office is administered by qualified and experienced Staff to ensure customer satisfaction.

The Company has a turnover in excess of £15m per annum and currently has some 850 employees, including apprentices, employed in any area of operations.

Contracts and orders undertaken from the smallest up to the largest value.

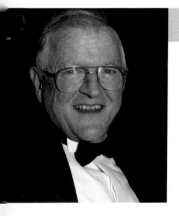

and played such a fundamental role in the Post War construction of the city. Throughout the Seddon community he stood as a respected, thoughtful manager of his staff.

At the Seddon Group Annual General Meeting, his son John paid tribute to a man admired across the company, from the building site to the boardroom, who had started work in the 1920s and played a major part in the family business right up until the 1980s.

The official opening of the Tytherington Golf Club took place in 1986 and the 18-hole course soon gained an excellent reputation, even hosting the Women's Professional Golf Association Competition three years later.

Brian Mellor, **(pictured above)**, is a retired member of staff who lives at Tytherington. Brian joined as a Company Secretary in 1980 – later becoming a Director - and went on to work for the company for 20 years. After his retirement in 2000, he stayed with Seddon as Chairman of the company's pension scheme.

More managerial changes came when, in 1987, Stuart Seddon was appointed a Director of the company. Bill Gibson, Clive Russell, Dave Povey and Jim Blairs were all appointed Divisional Directors.

The late eighties marked a period of great change at Seddon, but in October 1987, the company was in mourning after the death of Ernest Seddon – the man who had made the move by Seddon into Stoke possible

His death came at a time when the company recorded excellent results. In 1989, a record amount of £280,000 had been paid by Seddon (Stoke) in staff bonuses compared with £196,000 the previous year. An increase of eight per cent was awarded to hourly paid and salaried staff across the Group one year later. The minutes show that good results were posted across the Board during this time.

At this poignant period in the company's history, a major turning point occurred – which would transform the structure, ethos and approach of Seddon (Stoke). In September 1989, the first meetings of three new companies were held – J & S Seddon (Building) Ltd, J & S Seddon (Painting) Ltd, and Viceroy Developments.

All three companies would come under the control of Seddon (Stoke) Limited - and each given the resources and managerial expertise to grow under divisionalisation. Success was to come – but first the new companies had to negotiate the harsh times that marked the move from the 1980s into a new era as the recession started to bite.

Chapter 5

A Turbulent Time

Famine And Feast - The 1990s into The New Millennium

During the 20th Century, history shows the construction industry was hit hard in the 1930s, the early 1980s - and the early 1990s. The official formation of three subsidiary companies marked the beginning of the new decade – with J & S Seddon (Building) Ltd, J & S Seddon (Painting) Ltd and Viceroy Developments Ltd, all set-up on New Year's Day 1990.

However, their introduction came at a difficult time for Seddon (Stoke), with the 1990s among the toughest in its trading history. Redundancies, early retirements and cut-backs were all features of the era.

Margaret Thatcher resigned as Prime Minister in November 1990, at a time when Seddon started to put in place measures to protect the overall business as hard-times loomed on the horizon. Months earlier the Painting office, which moved premises from Hot Lane in Burslem to Fenton's Oldfield Business Park, had been forced to make redundancies.

Margaret Thatcher on the steps of Number 10 Downing Street, addressing the Press at the time of her resignation. Picture – Getty Images

Builder wields the jobs axe

ONE of Stoke-on-Trent's biggest building firms is to axe jobs - for the first time in its 95 year history.

The shock redundancies at Seddon Stoke Ltd which employs 850 workers were revealed today.

By Lesley Gerard

Managing director Mr John Seddon said the company was the latest victim of the crippling recession.

He said: "The company was established in 1897 and we have been based in the city since 1930. But this is the first time in our history we have had to lay-off staff for redundancy."

The cuts will hit office staff, builders and craftsmen.

"The construction industry has been badly affected by the recession and it has finally hit Seddon. There is a shortage of work and we have been unable to secure the contracts to keep us going at full strength,' he added.

He was unable to say exactly how many people face the axe.

"We have only just made the decision to make cutbacks. The first step is to see who will take early retirement and voluntary redundancy before we will know how many compulsory redundancies there will have to be.

"Seddon is an old family firm and we feel extremely sad it should come to this."

The company has depots in York, Newcastle-upon-Tyne and Cheltenham. Last year it had a £25 million turnover.

The bombshell comes just days after the closure of British Reinforced concrete at Stafford. Two hundred and sixty workers are now facing the dole.

Bosses blame the shut down on falling orders caused by the recession.

No-one from the construction unions was today available for comment.

Although good figures were being reported in the early 1990s, John Seddon and his team could see that trade 12 months into the future and beyond was going to become very difficult.

Company records in May 1991 go on to describe the situation as 'serious overall at Seddon (Stoke),' with all staff over the age of 60 offered early retirement.

Letters were sent to all hourly-paid employees working in the Building company warning about the 'very bad work situation' and what the company described as 'suicidal price rises.'

The Building company's regional office in Retford, Nottinghamshire, closed down. However, investment was poured into the Birmingham Building office, based in Perry Barr, which was refurbished and opened for use in its new capacity as a regional, rather than a site office.

In 1992, dinner dances were cancelled and the sheer number of redundancies and early retirements resulted in major changes in the office. Three of the company's long-serving Directors, Cyril Adams, Peter Mottram and Terry Smith also announced their plans for early retirement.

Better Times Loom

Although the company closed its plumbing and scaffolding departments early in 1993, later in that year company records show Seddon (Stoke) had started to pull through the recession, and was forming a 'strong and thriving business.' Looking back, John Seddon reported that *'1991 was probably the worst year of recession in his memory, and 1992 was as bad.'*

After getting through the hard times, there was the chance for celebration in May 1993. John's relatives and fellow Group directors, Christopher, David and George Seddon, presented him with an engraved claret jug and bottle of red wine to mark his 35 years as a Director of Seddon Holdings – now known as Seddon Group - the last 15 of which had been as Chairman.

Expansion On The Cards

Good figures and a reduction in the amount of cash outstanding provided the platform for growth in 1994. New Painting offices were proposed for Wrexham and Birmingham, with Andy Woodhouse and John Bentley appointed to lead the growth in these areas, while Bob Seers was tasked with expansion in the Cheltenham area.

John Wilburn became a Divisional Director in 1994 – leading Chester's Building office, which he had helped establish in 1985 as Office Manager, later becoming Area Manager. He had worked with Dave Povey, who had become a Divisional Director in the late 1980s with responsibility for Chester and

further afield. Dave was in charge of a number of successful measured term contracts throughout the 1960s, 70s and 80s across the company.

During the mid 1990s, fundamental changes in the company's leadership were set in place to ultimately put John's son Stuart Seddon in charge of Seddon (Stoke). Clive Russell took over as Joint Managing Director of the Painting company, along with Stuart, who was also made Chairman of the company.

John Seddon announced plans to reduce his role and gradually hand over to Stuart. As a result, he moved from offices in Duke Street, Fenton to Tytherington Old Hall – then headquarters of Seddon Group – in preparation for his looming retirement from Stoke operations.

managing the business, for John Seddon the challenge had been to get the company through the recessions that crippled the construction industry in the 1980s and then the early 1990s. Factors such as industry strikes and the three-day week, which blighted the 1970s, had presented additional challenges.

Many firms similar to Seddon folded in the midst of this hardship, but he successfully steered the company through the hard times, with an instinctive style that was based very much on leadership by example. At the time

Another significant change took place in 1995, with Jim Blairs appointed Joint Managing Director of the Building company, along with Stuart Seddon. Barry Thompson was also appointed a Director.

John Seddon Retires

John's grandfather, John Seddon senior, had to steer the company through two World Wars and the hardships of the 1930s. John's father, Ernest had to find a way of getting a new business off the ground from its Lancashire heartlands into North Staffordshire.

As a third generation member of the Seddon family

John Seddon hands over the reins as Chairman of Seddon Group to Rod Sellers OBE.

of his retirement, Seddon (Stoke) reported excellent figures – including the best ever recorded at the time for Painting – and a strong position overall for the company's future.

'Respected, meticulous, conscientious, thorough, a man of dignity,' a straw poll among staff asked to describe John Seddon's management style. One Building Manager recalls how he knew the name of each member of staff and sub-contractor working with the company – some 2,000 names in total.

John's modest approach meant that many people outside Seddon were unaware of the considerable role he played, not just in protecting and generating hundreds of jobs in Stoke-on-Trent and the rest of the UK, but within the community as a whole.

For years he served on the North Staffordshire Health Authority, and was a senior Governor of Stoke-on-Trent College for more than 20 years **(see Chapter Eight)**. John was also a Non-Executive Director of Britannia Building Society for 6 years. As Chairman of the North Staffordshire Joint Training Committee, John was asked in its centenary year to be chairman of the Construction Federation – a role he turned down after much deliberation in order to pursue a more leisurely retirement at the age of 65.

Still much-admired across the entire company, he remains a strong influence today in his role as a Non-Executive Director, more than 10 years after retiring as Managing Director.

In 1978, John had been made Chairman of Seddon Holdings – now known as Seddon Group Limited. He retired in 2006, handing over the reins to Rod Sellers OBE.

An Early Start

John signed his five-year apprenticeship deed aged 16, whilst still at school. At 17 youngsters were classed as too old to sign-up for the trade. The five-year term was then comparatively new and to the distaste of the old hands, who had served seven years.

As was the case for so many youngsters signing up to train for a trade, the signing ceremony was an important event in his life. His Uncle Frank was witness to the signing and his wife, John's Aunt Muriel, was also present. She challenged the teenager before he signed to become a bricklayer saying *'You do not know what you are letting yourself in for. You will be as bad as them, spending all your time at work,'* referring to his father Ernest, and his Uncle Frank.

Despite his Aunt Muriel's reservations, John set a strategy in place to leave school as soon as he possibly could, and start his training in Technical Building Studies at Stoke-on-Trent College, then moving to Salford's Royal Technical College.

John Seddon, pictured in 2006 at St Chad's Church, RAF Stafford. John led the construction project on site during the early 1960s.

A New Business Model

The mid-1990s ushered in a new way of doing business in the construction sector, which ultimately led to a more dynamic, customer-focused and professional industry.

Around this time, the Private Finance Initiative (PFI) emerged from the Government, to carry out their programme of capital works. Seddon set in place measures to take on this new style of contract.

Environmental issues also started to come to the fore, with an idea for a brochure on the subject muted at Group level.

Earlier in the late 1980s through to the early 1990s, there had been a proliferation of new regulations, which were changing the face of construction. These included COSHH, which focused on care in the use of hazardous substances, and hard hat regulations, which demanded a greater level of safety clothing on site. Noise regulations also came into force. All these changes, along with a consideration for the environment, Equal Opportunities and Quality Assurance procedures - signalled the start of greater professionalism and a uniform approach to better standards across the UK construction industry.

It was around this time that a report was produced for the construction sector, which was to ultimately change the entire workings of the industry – Sir Michael Latham's report, released in 1994, entitled 'Constructing the Team.' A joint industry – government report, it was based on the simple concept that through teamwork the construction industry could make significant improvements and efficiencies for its customers.

It acted as the catalyst for change in the industry. As well as setting the agenda for reform, The Latham Report gave the industry targets and from this a raft of initiatives flowed. The report led to the establishment of the Construction Industry Board to oversee reform. Subsequent initiatives included Sir John Egan's 1998 report 'Rethinking Construction', which called for increased productivity and reduced capital cost. From this, the concept of Partnering – the process of the client and contractor working together to achieve the highest standards - was put on the agenda. Seddon were well-placed to tap into this new type of business delivery.

The non-adversarial approach to the provision of its services had, in essence, been at the heart of the company business philosophy since its formation. Therefore, the move into formal Partnering/Best Value arrangements fitted the way the company had already been operating for almost a century.

A new main entrance under construction by Seddon at the Stafford campus of Staffordshire University. A large lecture theatre was also built.

At an event organised by G & J Seddon in 2005, Sir Michael Latham, pictured at the centre of this picture, met up with their apprentices at the Reebok Stadium for a presentation evening. More than 40 apprentices attended, as well as guests and Directors of G & J Seddon and Seddon Group.

Brighter Times

Already by 1996, a report in *The Sentinel* described how the Building company had enjoyed an 18 per cent growth in business, turning over £24 million, with five regional offices.

In the article, Painting had a turnover of £10 million and 12 regional branch offices. Managing Director, Clive Russell described how *'the company's rise in recent years, despite difficult times, was down to a combination of service and efficiency.'*

Finally, the article outlined how Viceroy Developments, under the Directorship of Kevin Edwards, had undertaken major works to reclaim and develop the 10-acre former brickworks – now known as Oldfield Business Park, as well as the expansion of Stone Business Park under a joint venture for Staffordshire County Council.

Two years later the regions were again under the spotlight in a report to staff from John Seddon in 1998. It reported growth for the Painting company in South Wales, York, Bristol, Southampton, Leicester and Birmingham and revealed the Building company had completed 118 projects, with a reasonable workload in the bag for 1999.

Despite this optimism in the marketplace, margins were still tight. John described that *'the profits of yesteryear have disappeared from the industry for good. It seems sometimes that our competitors, even during busy periods, have forgotten how to include profit whilst pricing for a job.'*

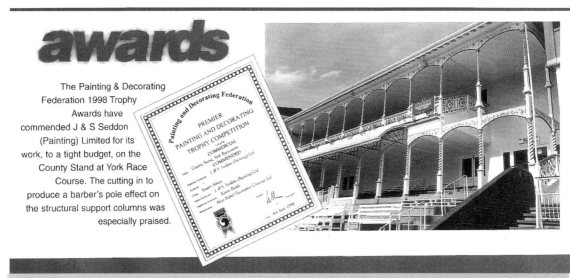

awards

The Painting & Decorating Federation 1998 Trophy Awards have commended J & S Seddon (Painting) Limited for its work, to a tight budget, on the County Stand at York Race Course. The cutting in to produce a barber's pole effect on the structural support columns was especially praised.

A report from the December 1998 edition of *Seddon News* about the Painting company's award success.

Ultimately, the 1990s marked a period of consolidation, a battle against the recession in the early years, and then a process of building the business up and using its strong position as a springboard for growth into the future.

A more positive outlook abounded in the late 1990s. The new Millennium was approaching – and for Seddon the hard times of the last decade were about to give way to a new era of major growth and business success that was to put the company firmly on the map as a key player in the UK's construction, maintenance and painting sectors.

Seddon builders, led by Hefin Edward's contract team, installed an oil interceptor at RAF Valley in Anglesey, measuring around 24 metres in length, by more than three metres in diameter, making it one of the largest installed in Europe at the time, in 1998. The interceptor was put in place to ensure oil from the runway did not contaminate the coastal waters.

SSPDS opened in 1997, to supply the Painting company, the trade and public, at Fenton Industrial Estate. It has carved out a niche for stocking a large product range, which serves the needs of the professional and DIY customer.

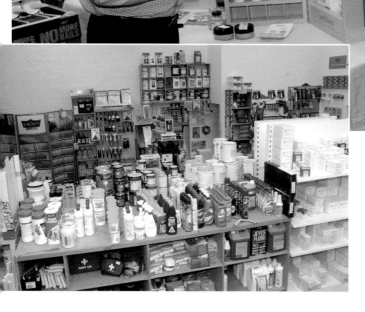

Explosive Times and High Action

Army blows up old grenade

By Scott Hamilton
Photos: Malcolm Hart

ARMY bomb disposal experts carried out a controlled explosion yesterday after shocked builders found an unexploded hand grenade.

Police rushed to evacuate the site and cordon off Muswell Road, off Etruria Road, Etruria, after a call from contractors.

And workmen watched from a distance as bomb squad experts stacked sandbags around the grenade before detonating it — hurling earth and debris 30 feet into the air.

J and S Seddon contracts manager Cyril Wakefield said: "The lads were just hand digging when they found the grenade.

"We had already dug over most of the site with machinery so this was a shock."

"We did have to stop work for a few hours but that was better than someone getting hurt."

Police believe the hand grenade was a World War Two relic overlooked when the site was part of Shelton Bar steelworks.

Very rusty

A police spokesman said: "The grenade was very rusty and in poor condition and had obviously been underground since the war."

"The contractors did exactly the right thing. They cleared the site and waited for us.

"Whenever we find a suspicious device we just cordoned off the site and wait for the experts. Sometimes they blow it up and sometimes they just take it away in bucket."

●Bomb disposal experts set a charge

Century Retail Park, on the outskirts of Hanley, was a major project for Seddon in the 1990s. It hit the headlines when the Bomb Squad (**pictured at the top of the page**) was called out on site to deal with an old grenade, and carried out a controlled explosion (**pictured below**).

●Blasted . . . the Army bomb disposal experts blow up the old grenade found in Etruria as workmen watch

The story was reported by The Sentinel.

Pictures courtesy of Cyril Wakefield, newspaper cutting courtesy of The Sentinel

An explosion of a different kind damaged one of Stoke's landmark buildings – and Seddon were called in to action repairs. The pottery company Moorcroft called out the company on a Sunday morning after lightning struck the bottle kiln – just days before their popular annual sale.

More work for a world-leading pottery manufacturer, Wedgwood's Global Distribution Centre built by Seddon in Stone, South Staffordshire, in the 1990s.

Moving Into The South West

Wotton Hill from The Chipping.

A historical picture of Jotcham and Kendall, based in picturesque Wotton-under-Edge, in Gloucestershire, and a more recent photograph. The company has a well-deserved reputation for quality and craftsmanship and provided Seddon with a springboard for growth in the South West of England and into South Wales.

A major purchase occurred in July 1999, when Gloucestershire-based Jotcham and Kendall was bought by Seddon. A family-owned company since the 1600s, Jotcham and Kendall became a trading division of J & S Seddon (Building) under the deal.

For centuries the company has been involved in building activities around the Gloucestershire area, which blend in with the unique character and style of the region. Work first started with the conversion of the Church House of St James Church, Charfield, in 1680.

Wotton Building Supplies (WBS), which is situated next to Jotcham and Kendall, was also purchased as part of the deal, with J & S Seddon (Painting) responsible for the management of the business.

Steve Owen (pictured) is the Director in charge of Jotcham and Kendall, supported by Geoff Major, the Company's Divisional Director.

The team from Wotton Building Supplies.

Recent Jotcham and Kendall projects include Bicester Barracks **(pictured above)** and The Dower House, situated on the outskirts of Bristol **(pictured below)**.

Mick Triner

Seddon's ability to retain staff was reflected in 2000, when 21 members of staff received Long Service Awards. They went to Brian Mellor, Kevin Crompton, Hefin Edwards, Wilfred Ireland, John Edwards, Paul Ellis, Dennis Bailey, Glenn Jennings, Peter Middleton, Lance Bickerton, Neil Hand, Garry Phillips, Andrew Woodhouse, Ian Gibson, Russell White, Martin Alexander, Peter Eaton, Steve Hand, David Moulton, John Emlyn Owen and Kenneth Roberts.

The New Millennium

The Building company kicked off the new century with its largest contract at the time, estimated at around £14 million, for the Defence Housing Executive. Following an intensive period of presentations, interviews, tender and quality plan submissions, the company was accepted as the contractor for the Western Region – stretching from Carlisle to Cardiff, including Wales and into the Midlands. One of the first jobs was to upgrade 160 houses over a 60 week period, at MOD Weeton, near Blackpool – a project carried out by the Chester Building office under the leadership of John Wilburn. A team, including Mick Triner **(pictured above)**, now the Director of Building's North Wales office in Flintshire worked on the DHE projects.

In *Seddon News*, Neil Cooke, Lee Painter, Steve Potter, Cyril Wakefield, Robert Brunt, Dave Kelly, John Hallam, Alan Brain, Kevin Crompton, Peter McKenna, Mick MacDonald, Darren Bowkett, Phil Hawkes, Keith Harris, Ian Gibson, Stan Bird, Ian Wright, Paul Birch, Darren Mills and Kevin Shutt were all singled out for praise for receiving letters of compliments from satisfied customers.

The education sector continued to expand in 2000 for both Building and Painting companies, with Seddon's flexible and fast approach helping to win new work. One project for Painting's Leicester office included the redecoration of student accommodation at Coventry University - completed in just 6 weeks.

In the North West, Stuart Seddon took a trip down Memory Lane in 2001, when the Headmaster of Mostyn House School asked the company to paint the building, situated on The Wirral. Stuart had been a pupil at the school, as well as his father John, Uncles George and Christopher and cousin Stephen Seddon. The painting project went on to reach the short list of the Painting and Decorating Federation's Annual Award.

Mark Holden, left, is pictured with Stuart Seddon and Clive Russell – who held the position of Joint Managing Director of 4m up to his retirement in 2006. This picture was taken to mark the acquisition.

Taking To The Floor

In 2002, Seddon (Stoke) expanded into a new market sector, with the acquisition of 4m flooring uk.

Under the leadership of the company's Managing Director, Mark Holden and fellow directors Andrew James and Kurt Singleton **(pictured below)**, 4m has carved out a niche as a top-flight provider in the design, installation and supply of commercial and industrial flooring for clients across the United Kingdom, the Republic of Ireland and the rest of Europe. The new deal provided the necessary support and stability to enable the company to grow further.

Since then 4m has gone from strength-to-strength in the marketplace. High profile projects, including installations at Vauxhall Motors, Dublin Airport, Ascot Racecourse, Jaguar and Bentley Motors have put it firmly on the map as the UK's leading flooring contractor. In 2006, the company secured the prestigious Specialist Contractor of the Year award, from *Building* magazine.

Another deal in 2003 saw the Painting company complete the purchase of Dennis Kehoe (Contracts) Limited, of Preston. The company specialised in the ecclesiastical and heritage sector, renowned for its expertise in high class work such as gilding, marbling, graining and frescos. The deal, which saw Vaughan Cartwright and Andy Woodhouse overseeing the smooth integration of the two companies, gave Seddon a foothold into a new niche market and a presence generally in the North West.

Kurt Singleton, Andrew James and Mark Holden of 4m.

Mark Holden, centre, receives the Specialist Contractor Awards, Flooring Category, organized by *Building* magazine.

4m floors at Bentley Motors, Jaguar, RAF Cottesmore and Ascot Racecourse.

Examples of some of the intricate work carried out by Dennis Kehoe in the ecclesiastical sector.

Big Deals

In 2002, J & S Seddon (Building) secured a major deal – a £16 million contract to refurbish Keele University's student accommodation. Undertaken under Partnering principles, the six-year contract led to a range of innovative methods being introduced on site, including the Construction Lean Improvement Programme, where methods of working have been closely reviewed to ensure the highest levels of performance.

At the same time, J & S Seddon (Painting) took on a series of major Partnering contracts. A £1.9 million, five-year deal with North British Housing was signed to carry out work to 5,000 properties in East and South Yorkshire. Later, the company secured more work to paint 5,000 homes in North and West Yorkshire. Since then, the contract with North British Housing has gone from strength to strength, covering a wider area of the UK.

Seddon has worked closely with North British Housing – part of the Places For People Group - on initiatives including the support of a DVD, promoting a positive approach to community life, sent to more than 50,000 North British Housing and New Leaf households across the UK.

Hot on the heels of the North British Housing deal, the Painting company signed another Partnering contract with Hanover Housing Association, based in West Yorkshire, for 3749 homes across Yorkshire, Lancashire, Cumbria, Teeside, Durham and Tyneside.

Providing high levels of student accommodation under a Partnering contract at Keele University.

Representatives from the Painting company and Hanover Housing Association at a contract meeting.

Representatives from the Painting company and Hanover Housing Association at a contract meeting.

This was followed by a five-year deal with Trent and Dove Housing. Involving thousands of homes across East Staffordshire, the £2 million, five-year programme was secured after the company successfully undertook a pilot programme with the Burton-based housing association. J & S Seddon (Painting) created a new depot in Burton to deliver the works programme.

In 2003, the Building company signed its largest contract to date, a Partnering agreement with long-standing client Staffordshire Country Council. The five-year project involves Seddon working alongside the Authority's Property and Estates Division to carry out maintenance and minor construction works.

A new team – led by Kevin Wood and assisted by Bob Brunt and Mike Swindells – moved to offices in Stafford to handle the project. The contract has been one of the major successes in the Seddon story to date.

Steve Greaves, who works for the Painting company enjoys a well-earned cuppa from a Trent and Dove resident.

Signing up for the deal with Trent and Dove Housing Association.

The project with Staffordshire County Council has included works to create high-class facilities for schools in the area, with educational establishments being a fundamental part of the contract. It has also led to Seddon implementing their first ever Servicing and Testing contract, to monitor and maintain a significant number of the Authority's services including fire alarms, air conditioning, water hygiene and other factors, under the management of the Seddon Servicing and Testing Manager Elizabeth Walters.

Kevin Wood, a Director of J & S Seddon (Building), with responsibility for the Staffordshire County Council contract. Kevin is also in charge of the Derby and Normanton offices.

Seddon employee Neil Fraser, pictured far right, who works as a Quality and Environment Manager, has pioneered a number of 'green' initiatives, including an environmental handbook for site staff.

The Company Today

Today, Seddon (Stoke) has come a long way since its official registration 50 years ago. The company has enjoyed significant growth - built on its core, family-held principles, which have been maintained through thick and thin.

A diverse portfolio of work, well-trained, courteous staff and a first-rate, consistently high quality service to clients are the hallmarks of Seddon in the 21st Century.

The company's business philosophy - centred around an open, honest approach - is now regarded as best practice in the industry, and the company is seen as one of the leading exponents of the delivery of contracts based on the Partnering ethos.

Delivering Excellence

Under the direction of Stuart Seddon, the company has pioneered a number of initiatives which set a benchmark for excellence in the industry on a national level.

These include Seddon Business Solutions, a programme set up by the company where staff meet regularly and discuss a specific aspect of the business operation, look at ways to improve it, and action those improvements.

Environment and sustainability are also at the top of the agenda. Seddon was one of the first construction companies to achieve the standard ISO 14001, and there is a focus on achieving environmental excellence across all operations of the business.

J & S Seddon (Painting) Managing Directors, Neil Hand and Mark Brindley. In 2006, the company marked a new era, with the retirement of Clive Russell (pictured above) as Managing Director and a move into new high-technology offices in Oldfield Business Park. Neil and Mark are supported by Regional Directors, Alan Liddell and Chris Pritchard. Clive Russell remains a Non-Executive Director of Seddon (Stoke).

Any company is only as good as its staff. The company's commitment to training, pioneered by Ernest Seddon, nurtured by John Seddon and expanded and developed by Stuart Seddon, continues to be the major policy at the core of the business.

A New Approach At Bentilee

Seddon (Stoke's) first PFI contract for the multi-million pound Bentilee Neighbourhood District Centre showed the company's ability to undertake large-scale construction projects – and its commitment to community involvement.

J & S Seddon (Building) carried out the building work at the Bentilee Neighbourhood Centre, on behalf of Regenter, the equity investor and project manager. Regenter is an investor in social housing and community based PFI projects. The building was designed by architects Hulme Upright Manning.

A joint initiative between Stoke-on-Trent City Council and Stoke-on-Trent Primary Care Trust, the new centre – completed in 2007 - brings together a broad range of services, including healthcare and housing, and a local authority 'One Stop Shop,' all under the same roof. A community hall has also been created for local use, as well as retail outlets.

The work – managed by Seddon's Warren Smith, under the directorship of Barry Thompson, (**pictured opposite**) - was completed on time and within budget. J & S Seddon (Building) are now responsible for the facilities management at the centre.

Donna Hall, Personal Assistant to the Painting company's Managing Directors, at the new offices.

Pictured in 2006, the then Stoke-on-Trent Lord Mayor Maurice Lewis carries out a Topping Out Ceremony at the site.

Barry Thompson, Director of the Building company's Stoke regional office.

Local schoolchildren plant a time capsule at the Bentilee Neighbourhood Centre.

Seddon staff help retailers move from the old site of Devonshire Square in Bentilee, into a temporary retail village, until they were able to move into the new centre.

Quadrant since August 2005 – the largest contract secured by the company to date - which involves more than 17,500 properties.

London & Quadrant included its own training initiative, entitled STEP (Supported Training & Education Pathway), in the project, to create training opportunities in painting and decorating for its residents.

A Blueprint For Painting Contracts

Pioneering initiatives such as employing residents as trainees and continuously improving performance secured J & S Seddon (Painting) a prestigious award from London & Quadrant Housing Trust in 2007.

The company was named Maintenance Contractor of the Year at the London & Quadrant Maintenance Awards.

J & S Seddon (Painting) has been working on the innovative £10 million partnering contract with London &

Working Well Together

Seddon has built up close working relations with suppliers and clients across the UK.

The Painting company works closely with paint and product manufacturers including Akzo Nobel, ICI Dulux and STO, to deliver professionally applied products that stand the test of time.

Tinsdills, based in Stoke-on-Trent, have been valued solicitors to Seddon for decades. Michael Hand was the company's solicitor for almost 50 years. Richard Whitehouse **(pictured below left)** and Andrew Brian **(pictured below right)** now work closely with the company.

Workers from the Painting office's Airdrie office worked through the night to complete a contract at Waverley Station in Edinburgh for Christmas 2006.

Company Today
Project Round-up

Painters from the company's Birmingham office scaled the heights at tower blocks in Walsall, run by Leamore Tenant Management Organisation and owned by Watmos Community Homes.

Another high-rise project, painters from the Southampton office battled against the sea and the elements to complete a major project at the city's National Oceanography Centre.

Innovation At Bevan Lee

Seddon joined forces with Beth Johnson Housing Association to undertake one of the UK's most innovative social housing schemes. The project involves the demolition of sub-standard homes in Bevan Lee, Cannock and replacing them with modern properties that re-build a sense of community.

J & S Seddon (Building) is constructing the new homes. The total cost of the project is almost £15 million. The partnership also involves Cannock Chase District Council, who own the bulk of the homes on the estate.

Residents have been able to select the type of home they require, where it will be located within Bevan Lee and also a choice on the type of kitchen, bathroom and interior fittings.

Innovative ideas have been introduced including the creation of a new social enterprise business – Butty Angels **(pictured below)** - where two local women have set up their own catering business to supply meals to construction workers on site. Local youngsters have also been taken on as apprentices.

The Partnership team on site.

Butty Angels set-up to supply hungry construction workers with meals on site.

In 2007, J & S Seddon (Building) secured a £2.2 million contract to build the Claus Moser Research Centre at Keele University in Staffordshire. Pictured are Peter Wrench, J & S Seddon (Building) site manager, Alan Nixon, Managing Director of J & S Seddon (Building), John Tiernan of Pick Everard, Lord Moser and Brian Rule of Pick Everard.

Company Today
Project Round-up

Peter Hordley, of the Birmingham office of J & S Seddon (Building), pictured on the ground as a member of Bromsgrove District Council digs deep to mark the start of work to build Bromsgrove Arts Centre.

Ashby School in Leicester signed up to a new rolling maintenance programme with J & S Seddon (Painting). Pictured are Sean Butler of Seddon's Leicester office with Anita Allsop, Ashby School's Senior Administrator.

The Derby office of J & S Seddon (Building) signed up to a social housing scheme which will help regenerate the North East Derbyshire market town of Shirebrook for East Midlands Housing Association. East Midlands Housing's Regional Development Manager, Ailsa Daykin is pictured with Adam Williams of Seddon.

J & S Seddon (Painting) has pioneered the use of a range of innovative paints and other products, under the management of Philip Marsden. Here demonstrations of Graffiti Block take place at Maidstone (**pictured below**) and Mansfield (**pictured left**). The demonstrations were made to local authority and police representatives – and at Maidstone the event was reported by television, radio and newspapers in the region.

The Directors of J & S Seddon (Building), pictured in 2006 with Stuart Seddon, at the time of Alan Nixon's appointment as Managing Director. Alan took over from Jim Blairs (**pictured right**), who worked for the company for 41 years. He remains a Non-Executive Director. Left to right. Steve Owen, Kevin Wood, Stuart Seddon, Alan Nixon, Barry Thompson and Mick Triner.

The story so far - a slice of company history was marked on the 1st February 2007, as Seddon (Stoke) celebrated the 50th year of its registration. A cake themed on a Seddon van was baked by Staffordshire-based Amerton Bakery to mark the occasion. Weighing more than 70 pounds and measuring almost three feet in length, it took 35 hours to make and decorate, using 80 eggs and six kilos of icing.

Seddon The Story So Far

A celebration of 50 years of Seddon (Stoke) Ltd.

PART TWO

Company Culture

Part of the Seddon Group, Seddon Homes is noted for its prestigious new-build and refurbishment projects across the North and the Midlands. Several years ago, it moved into regeneration with the creation of Inspired Developments, which specialises in urban renewal in the residential and commercial property sectors.

A Seddon Homes development, luxury properties built to the highest specification.

A contemporary feel - the corporate identity of Inspired Developments.

id inspired developments

A *Seddon* Group Company

Chapter 6 A Family Focus

The Seddon Family And The Seddon Companies

Back in August 1978, Ernest Seddon gave a view of the past – and a vision of the future – as he addressed a meeting of Seddon Directors, when he resigned as Chairman of Seddon Holdings and his son John took over.

He reflected on how George Seddon, the co-founder of the company, had once told his brother - and fellow company co-founder - John Seddon Senior, that it was possible for brothers to work together, but not so for cousins.

But John Seddon disputed his brothers' viewpoint, and years later, Ernest, John's son, described at that meeting in the 1970s why he also shared the same view as his father – that the company's future lay in the hands of the family. Speaking to the Board, he said: *'We are now going to prove that cousins can work together, although it will need a lot of patience and tolerance, but it will be well worthwhile in the end. No competition need be feared and we have everything in front of us both to win and for the betterment of everyone who works in the firm.'*

George's children did not follow their father into the business – his son Fred chose a career in the Church – but John's children did, with Ernest, Frank and Jonas all going on to play a major role in the family company's growth and development.

In turn, their offspring, Christopher, George and John, also became great leaders and now their children – the fourth generation, known throughout Seddon as G4 - are showing that Ernest's view, set out at that Directors' meeting almost 30 years ago, was correct.

Two pictures of the co-founder, George Seddon, with his family. George was a man of great resolve and determination. Before the Great War of 1914, he journeyed around Essex and Ireland to make contacts and secure work. An insight into his strength of will is captured in a letter he wrote to his wife, while travelling. *'I am up before 6am, travelling many miles just to get a foot in, sometimes it is after 9pm before I can undo my boots. The work is challenging and I know that I shall succeed in getting orders and work for the men. Tell our John to buy those bricks, see you sometime before 10pm Friday.'*

A picture, taken in 1950 of John Seddon, the co-founder, with his wife Eliza. Pictured on the left are Ernest and Dora Seddon.

The superb headquarters of G & J Seddon, based in Bolton.

G2 and G3 A picture of the second and third generation. Left to right standing George, John, Christopher and David. Seated, Jonas, Arnold Hadley, Ernest and Frank.

G3 and G4 pictured together in 1995. Left to right, George, John, Stuart, Stephen, Jonathan, David and Christopher.

A later shot, which includes Ken Whitaker. From the back of the picture from left to right are George and Christopher. The next row from left to right are Stephen and Jonathan. At the front of the picture from left to right are Stuart and John with Ken Whitaker.

District Garage
SPECIALISTS
Tel: 01204 854670

Since 1957, Seddon (Stoke) has been a separate company from G & J Seddon, the founding company first created by George and John in the 1800s. However, Seddon (Stoke) and G & J Seddon are all part of the Seddon Group, managed by G4, which is now one of the largest family-owned construction companies in the UK.

As the Seddon Group of companies has developed over more than 100 years, with the Seddon family continuously at the helm, it's hard to imagine what George and John – the two orphans from Bolton who decided to leave the pits and 'go it alone' – would make today of the considerable role their family plays in the nation's construction, painting and maintenance industry.

District Garage is based in Smethurst Lane, Bolton and is noted across the North West for its excellent service. Carrying out vehicle sales, repairs and maintenance for a number of private and commercial clients, in 2004 it was named one of the best garages in the country after reaching the finals of the Independent Garage of the Year contest, at the national Motor Trader Industry Awards.

The Group Structure

There are 13 subsidiaries under the Seddon Group, but nine main business areas, which come under the control of the Board members; Stuart Seddon, Seddon (Stoke); Jonathan Seddon, G&J Seddon Construction; Stephen Seddon, Seddons (Plant & Engineers), Winget and District Garage; Ken Whitaker, Seddon Homes and Inspired Developments; and Board chairman Rod Sellers OBE. Rod became Chairman on John Seddon's retirement from the role in June 2006, which he had held for almost 30 years. Rod Sellers and Ken Whitaker are the only members of the Group Board who are not members of the Seddon family.

Rod Sellers OBE, Chairman of the Seddon Group

Seddons (Plant and Engineers) headquarters in Bolton. The company supplies plant and equipment to the construction, hire and groundcare industries and operates a network of regional depots.

One of the company's early vehicles

A group shot at the wedding of Ernest and
Dora Seddon.

Christopher Seddon celebrates a
topping out ceremony for a
bungalow built in Prestwich in
the 1960s.

Another group shot, taken in the late 1970s. This shows Ernest
Seddon's sons and daughters, and their families.

George and Stephen Seddon.

Christopher Seddon and his family, left to right Jonathan, Nicola and Jamie.

John Seddon's wife Claire, with their daughters Susan Nuttall and Helen Oakey. Helen is a director of Seddon Estates Limited.

Gold Service

At Seddon (Stoke), the major impact of being a family controlled business has been the stability and loyalty of the workforce.

It is not unusual for people to be with the company for 20 or 30 years. Instances of people working for the family for 40 and even 50 years are also on record.

A useful indication of the length of service enjoyed among workers is shown in the company minutes. In 1973, an incredible 58 gold watches were given to employees, who had been with the company for 21 years or more, and a further 21 watches awarded in 1975.

Even in more modern times, this long service culture is still evident. In 2005, Dave Sutton retired after clocking up 50 years with the company. His last day with Seddon was spent on site at Etruria, where the job he was working on was finished completely on time – on the day of his retirement.

Dave was offered a trip with his wife, anywhere around the world. However, Dave asked if he could have his trusted Seddon work van instead, which Stuart Seddon was more than happy to give to the loyal worker.

Ray Herbert served with the company for 51 years. He chose a trans-Atlantic visit to mark his retirement - unwittingly. John Seddon approached him as his final working days neared and asked him what his dream trip would be. Ray, never even thinking that the two could be linked, said a trip on Concorde to New York.

Ray was shocked and delighted to discover his retirement present included this remarkable trip to the Big Apple – for both him and his wife Margaret – with accommodation in a luxury hotel.

Dave Sutton with Stuart and John Seddon.

Ray Herbert, second right, receiving his gold watch for long service from Dora Seddon. Pictured second from left is Dennis Smith receiving his watch from Claire Seddon.

Family and friends gathered for Ray's retirement presentation.

Ray and Margaret on holiday in New York. Seddon sent the couple to the Big Apple on Concorde as a thank you for Ray's 51 years' service with the company.

More long service watch presentations. This picture shows George Field receiving his watch from Claire Seddon.

George, pictured here at work, served as a foreman joiner for many years.

Another gold watch presentation, to Wilf Cope and Jack Finney.

Steve Wood has clocked up 30 years' service with Seddon. He started out as an apprentice joiner and now works as a Site Agent, on projects across Staffordshire and Cheshire.

119

A Family Affair

Another factor associated with family management at Seddon (Stoke) is that, in turn, the number of families working at the company has flourished.

In 2006, records show that more than 40 people working for Seddon have relatives within the company, with many of the names being father and son relationships.

One example is that of Jack Hand, a well-respected member of the company's painting team, who retired in the mid 1990s after more than 40 years with the company. His wife, Nancy, also worked for Seddon, as a cleaner. His son, Dennis, worked as an apprentice and then tradesman plasterer for 10 years, joining in the 1960s. In the 1980s, Dennis's two children, Neil and Steve - Nancy and Jack's grandchildren - both joined the company - on the same day. The two youngsters joined as trainees and now Neil is joint Managing Director of the Painting company and Steve is Contracts Manager at the Nottingham Painting office.

Other examples include Ian Gibson – son of Bill Gibson, a former Painting company Divisional Director – who works at the York office. Dave Povey Jnr. – the son of Dave Povey, the retired Building company's Divisional Director in the 1980s and 90s – works as a Site Manager with Jotcham & Kendall, while Mike Swindells – son of Tony **(see page 151)**, works at Stafford's Building office.

Father and son John and Warren Smith, **(pictured opposite)**, both worked together on the Bentilee Neighbourhood Centre in 2005. Warren was Contracts Manager for the project.

Another father and son team is Chris Pritchard, **(pictured opposite)**, and his son Matthew. Chris joined as a painter and decorator in the early 1990s working at Cheltenham. He was made a Regional Director, based from the Stoke-on-Trent head office, in 2005. Around the time of his promotion, Chris's son Matthew joined as a trainee painter, working out of the company's Cheltenham office.

Steve and Neil Hand.

Warren and John Smith on site at the Bentilee Neighbourhood Centre which started in 2005 Warren was Contracts Manager for this development, a major multi-million pound project for the company. John also worked on the site.

Chris and Matthew Pritchard.

Brother and sister Claire and James Parsonage, pictured left in this photograph, both work for Seddon in Birmingham, at the Building company. Here they are being filmed for a DVD about the benefits of working for a family firm.

Brothers Nathan and Matthew Stevenson both work for the company. Matthew, pictured left, is a Painting Foreman and Nathan works as an Administration Manager at Seddon (Stoke's) Duke Street office.

John Bentley retired from the Birmingham Painting office after 35 years' service. He started work for Seddon in 1970 as a Painter and Decorator for the Chester Painting office. He went on to become Foreman Painter and then Painting Agent. In 1997 he became Storeman at Birmingham's Painting office, where he remained until his retirement in 2005.

John Bentley's son Phil, is the Manager of SSPDS, a Seddon company, which supplies paint and associated materials to the trade and public from a retail site in Fenton.

Father and son, Garry and James Phillips. Garry is an Area Manager at the Birmingham Painting office and James – 2006 Apprentice of the Year – works from Stoke as a trainee painter.

Mother and son, Julie and Alex Brough – Alex is a Trainee Joiner and Julie provides PA cover to the Financial Controller and Company Secretary.

Wedding Bells

Seddon has also played cupid to a number of couples who have worked for the company and then gone on to tie the knot.

Peter Mottram first met his wife, Carol, in the office. They are pictured on the far right of this photograph.

Derek Ward and his wife June, pictured on their wedding day. Derek worked for many years as John Seddon's assistant, while June worked in accounts and wages.

Kevin and Lisa Wakefield, pictured centre, got married after meeting at Seddon's Duke Street office. Kevin is now the company's Cost and Payroll Manager, and Lisa left her job as an Accounts Clerk to look after their two young daughters, Chloe and Amy. Kevin is the nephew of Cyril Wakefield, pictured right, Building Manager at Seddon (Stoke). Lisa's father, Richard Foster, pictured left, worked for Seddon in Stoke for more than 30 years as a Building Foreman. Richard is now a Building Manager for Seddon Homes. Both Cyril and Richard went to college together as young trainees at the beginning of their careers with the company.

The Seddon Group corporate identity drawn up to mark 100 years.

A Century Celebration

In 1997, The Seddon Group celebrated its centenary year. A series of events were held to mark the occasion with employees from all companies within the Group taking part.

The major celebration was a huge family party, based on a circus theme, under a giant top marquee. Held for all involved with the company, the sun shone down on the party, which took place at Arley Hall near Northwich.

Ken Dodd made a guest appearance in the evening. Throughout the day everyone enjoyed an action-packed agenda, including music, funfair rides, football tournaments, clowns, circus acts and an It's A Knockout style competition.

As well as the big party, members of the Seddon family also had a celebration at Loch Lomond.

A staff party was also held at the Piccadilly Plaza in Manchester. At the event, a 100-year-old bottle of port was opened to mark the occasion.

Ken Dodd at The Seddon Group centenary celebration party.

Stuart Seddon shakes hands with another contestant in the It's A Knockout style event.

The football tournament.

Invitation

SEDDON FAMILY CENTENARY WEEKEND

We request the pleasure of your company at Cameron House Hotel, Loch Lomond, for the weekend of 16th to 18th May 1997

RSVP before 28th February to: Seddon Group Ltd (Centenary Family Weekend), The Old Hall, Tytherington, Macclesfield, Cheshire SK10 2LQ

The invitation sent out to Seddon family members for the 100 year celebration at Loch Lomond.

Harold Donnelly and John Seddon with a 100-year-old bottle of port.

A group shot of the Seddon family at the Scottish party.

Chapter 7

Parties, Humour and Sense of Community

Company Life In Stoke-on-Trent And Further Afield

From the earliest days, at the core of the Seddon philosophy there has been a commitment to the welfare of its staff, and support to the needs of the wider community.

Over the years, this has helped to create a sociable culture that runs throughout the company.

Good causes are supported, workers and their families are helped in times of need - and colleagues come together to enjoy each others' company in their leisure time.

Seddon Social

For many Seddon staff the company's annual dinner dances, held around Christmas time, are a major highlight in the social calendar.

The Seddon parties started to emerge in the 1950s, around the time the restrictions from the Second World War were being lifted.

Although the parties began in the 1950s, trips and events were commonplace years before. This photograph was taken in the 1940s and shows Ernest Seddon taking aim during a visit to Blackpool.

For Seddon (Stoke), the North Stafford Hotel was often the venue for the annual dinner dance events. Occasionally, regional offices in York and Anglesey would hold celebrations in their own areas, mainly due to the travel involved in getting to The Potteries for the festivities.

A party in Anglesey (above) and in York (right).

Another party in 1957, John Seddon's stag night, held at The Rudyard Hotel, near Leek, in Staffordshire, where workfriends enjoyed a pint and a sing song.

The dinner dances in the 1950s were fairly formal affairs – but this was a reflection of the social make-up of the time rather than company policy. Couples had to be married – or at least engaged – to go along to an event together. Times have changed and now such restrictions are no longer in place.

Party games used to be an important part of the festive events. Too much Christmas spirit might have had an effect on the steady hand and cool head needed to play games such as these pictured here, fishing for bottles and wool wrapping races.

Evelyn, wife of George Grocott, would often sing at Seddon annual dinner dances, along with Fred Smith. Both had superb voices and Ernest Seddon started the tradition by asking them to sing a duet at the events, to the delight of the crowd.

As well as staff, in the 1950s and 1960s, employees' youngsters were also well catered for by the company. The green Seddon buses would journey across North Staffordshire, collecting the children of company workers for the Seddon Children's Christmas Party. A magnificent spread of food, a visit from Father Christmas and gifts to take away made the annual event — held at Longton Town Hall — a magical experience.

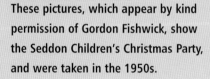

These pictures, which appear by kind permission of Gordon Fishwick, show the Seddon Children's Christmas Party, and were taken in the 1950s.

SEDDON (STOKE) LIMITED

Annual Dinner Dance

NORTH STAFFORD HOTEL, STOKE-ON-TRENT
SATURDAY, 8th JANUARY, 1977

Cocktails 7.00 p.m.   Dinner 7.30 p.m.

This menu card from Seddon Stoke's annual dinner dance in 1977, held at the North Stafford Hotel, shows that staff enjoyed a starter of quiche Lorraine, French onion soup, then steak and vegetables, all finished with Black Forest gateau.

Tastes have changed, but the annual dinner dances have held their place as popular events within the company.

Here and over the next five pages, are images from Seddon (Stoke) parties across the decades.

Seddon
Parties

Seddon
Parties

Seddon
Partie

Seddon
Parties

A New Era

Images from the 2005 Christmas parties, held over two nights – one for the Building company and the other for the Painting company and 4m flooring uk.

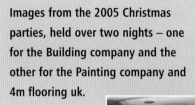

Celebrating Half a Century

To mark the 50th anniversary of Seddon (Stoke) in 2007, the entire company came together with a spectacular celebration event at the International Convention Centre, in Birmingham. Organised by Lindsay Baggaley, the party was the first time Seddon held its annual dinner dance outside North Staffordshire – reflecting the changing national focus of the company.

Partying at the 2007 50th anniversary celebration. The event included a casino for Seddon staff to try their hand at roulette and Black Jack.

Lindsay Baggaley with Stuart Seddon.

Stuart Seddon, pictured at the party, with his wife Maxine.

Seddon Giftware

As a community-based employer, Seddon has utilized the skill base of the local area to mark special occasions within the company.

In particular, as a Potteries-based firm, Seddon (Stoke) has involved local pottery firms to produce mementoes for key events in the company's history.

This trinket box **(pictured above)**, made by Heron Fine China, was given to all ladies attending the Christmas party of Seddon (Stoke) in 1982 - the company's Silver Jubilee year. An ashtray **(pictured below)** was presented to male members of staff.

This tankard was made by Crown Staffordshire and commissioned by Seddon upon the completion of flats in Hanley, along Bucknall New Road. It was presented to men on site and other people involved in the high-rise project. Jack Hood, pictured left in 2006, the Clerk of Works on the programme, donated his to the Potteries Museum and Art Gallery.

To mark the centenary of Seddon Group in 1997, the company approached Aynsley to produce a decorative dish. All female members of staff received this as a gift to mark the 100 year celebration. Here (**pictured below**), a card from John Seddon was written to his mother Dora, along with her gift.

Crystal was used by Seddon to celebrate the same occasion for male members of staff. These whisky glasses were given to men at the company, as their commemorative gift. The glasses were made by Stuart Crystal, who also produced a Seddon ashtray, which was given to customers and others associated with the company.

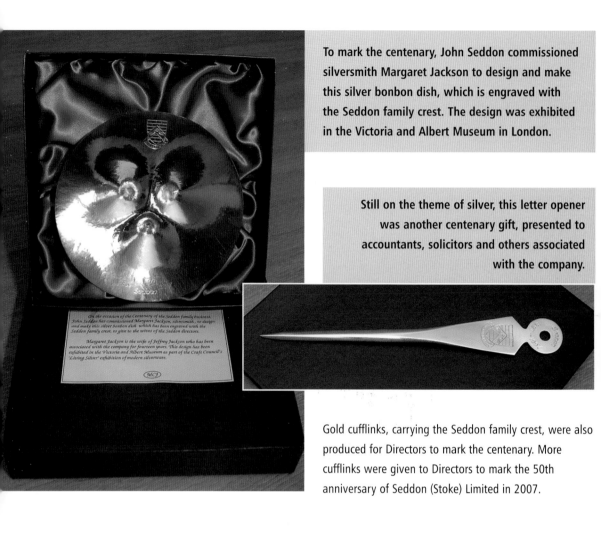

To mark the centenary, John Seddon commissioned silversmith Margaret Jackson to design and make this silver bonbon dish, which is engraved with the Seddon family crest. The design was exhibited in the Victoria and Albert Museum in London.

Still on the theme of silver, this letter opener was another centenary gift, presented to accountants, solicitors and others associated with the company.

Gold cufflinks, carrying the Seddon family crest, were also produced for Directors to mark the centenary. More cufflinks were given to Directors to mark the 50th anniversary of Seddon (Stoke) Limited in 2007.

Company Involvement in the Community

The team from Seddon (Stoke) pictured at Stoke City Football Club, where the company signed up to a deal in 2006 to sponsor the Waddington Suite, at the Britannia Stadium. On the far right of the picture is Johan Boskamp, the then manager of SCFC, and next to him one of the side's best known players from its glory days in the 1970s, Terry Conroy.

Across the UK, community-based projects have been supported by Seddon (Stoke). A small selection of good causes supported in 2006 included;

Stafford Building Office
Cannock Town Junior Football Team

York Painting Office
Montague and North Fenham Junior Football Club, Newcastle-upon-Tyne

North Tees Golf Day – cash for prizes

Cumberland Infirmary Charity Day - cash for prizes

Broadacres Housing Association Golf Day - cash for prizes

Newcastle-upon-Tyne Police Authority to Romanian children – gifts of t-shirts, polo shirts and paint

Airdrie Painting Office
Manor Estates Housing Association

Castle Rock Housing Association

Local football team

Christmas hampers for the elderly

Southampton Painting Office
Warsash Wasps – kit for the all-girl football team

Blackbrook Maternity Hospital – Funds to help purchase special pillowcases for newborn babies

Jotcham & Kendall
Gloscat (Gloucester College of Arts & Technology) – cash towards the annual building department prize-giving

The British School – a donation of top-soil for the children's garden

Leicester Painting Office
Ashby School – sponsored the drama department and bought new kit for the hockey team

Copies of
Seddon News.

In The News

In a company as geographically diverse as Seddon, communication is a key factor. For around ten years, *Seddon News* has been produced by the company to keep people abreast of the latest goings-on. The magazine is also sent to retired staff. Lindsay Baggaley has edited the publication for the last five years, taking over from the previous editor, Margaret Whitehouse.

Lindsay Baggaley, editor of
Seddon News.

cheltenham office

" It was the best experience anybody could ever have, although I was very nervous, I have now fulfilled my lifelong ambition to be on television and would recommend it to everyone".

On Friday 26th May 2000 the team from Cheltenham Office travelled by minibus with friends and family to Yorkshire Television in Leeds to take part in two shows of "Bruce's Price is Right".

On arrival at the studios, we were all ushered into the large canteen area and issued with our name badges. The show has an audience capacity of approx. 760 people and as you can imagine the waiting room was very busy with an intoxicating buzz of excitement.

Then our team was called by the audience entertainer, this was our cue to enter the studio and take our seats, but before that we all stood in groups of four in front of the programmes producers and tried to impress them with our smiles as it is at this stage they pick the contestants.

For the first show, we all had seats at the very back of the studio and although we were slightly disheartened by this, the appearance of Bruce Forsyth and the show that followed more than compensated. Every time the cameras started scanning for the next contestant we held our breath with anticipation.

Even though none of our group had been called down for the first show, we all enthusiastically cheered on the other contestants.

During the break after the first show's recording, Bruce entertained the audience by tap dancing, stand up comedy and questions from the audience.

Before the start of the second show, to our surprise and amazement the Floor Manager moved various groups to different locations in the studio and luckily enough our group was seated in the second row directly behind contestants row in the vision of the stage floor cameras.

The Producer informed us that because we were going to be in shot for the majority of the show and that it was important that our enthusiasm was at its maximum. Not that we needed telling this because our excitement got the better of us.

The first four contestants of the second show were chosen and the winner of that heat moved onto an individual game leaving a space in contestant's row.

To the delight of Angie Wherry the Secretary at Cheltenham Office, she was next to be called to "Come on down". Our group erupted into a frenzy of cheers as Angie made her way down the stairs to take her place on contestant's row. After some bizarre show of excitement Bruce greeted Angie by saying "Calm down girl, you'll do yourself an injury".

She then had to price the first item, which was a swinging garden seat, unfortunately she bid too high. The last chance to get to the next round had come and she had to bid for a leather hippo footstool, she then made a bid of £275.00 but unfortunately the right price was £240.00. Angie and the remaining contestants then took their places back in the audience.

At the end of the show, all the contestants called down were invited to have their photograph taken with Bruce and the models. Angie then asked if the whole group could have a photo taken and Bruce obliged.

This show is being televised on Saturday 16th December 2000 at 7.00pm on ITV

Angie quoted " It was the best experience anybody could ever have, although I was very nervous, I have now fulfilled my lifelong ambition to be 'on television and would recommend it to everyone"

Finally, Chris Pritchard, Regional Manager quoted "The whole experience was a great team building exercise and has proved that my team can work together in and out of working hours and would not hesitate in doing something similar again".

"come on down"

8

Seddon News **reports on the new TV stars - Cheltenham Painting office, pictured with Bruce Forsyth.**

To the delight of Angie Wherry, who worked as a secretary at the office, her name was called out by Bruce, to take her place in contestant's row. Unfortunately Angie came away empty-handed, but she managed to arrange a picture of the Cheltenham painting team with Bruce.

Heart Start Programme

In 2003, the Lord Mayor of Stoke-on-Trent, Mr Ellis Bevan, officially opened the Seddon Training Centre, situated off Victoria Road in Fenton. At the opening John Seddon pledged to provide £3,000 to the Lord Mayor's Charity Fund, from Seddon Group Charitable Trust, to purchase a heart defibrillator.

The Lord Mayor made a return visit to Seddon, to the Duke Street head office, along with Tony Berry, chairman of the North Staffs Heart Committee, to see how the defibrillator worked and receive the life-saving equipment from John Seddon.

Cheltenham Office – Come On Down

In May 2000, the team from Cheltenham office made the trip to Leeds to join the audience for the game show "Bruce's Price Is Right." As part of the high energy show, Bruce Forsyth would shout several names of people in the audience, inviting them to 'come on down.' to the stage and compete for expensive prizes such as cars and luxury holidays.

> John Seddon presents a life-saving heart-start machine to Mr Ellis Bevan, the Lord Mayor of Stoke-on-Trent in 2003. The picture also shows the Lady Mayoress, Seddon (Stoke) Directors and Tony Berry, chairman of the North Staffs Heart Committee.

An example of just one of the many reports that have appeared in *Seddon News* over the years regarding the prowess of Seddon staff on the football pitch. This particular article focuses on the rivalry between the Building company's football team, and the rival Painting team at a match played in 2000. Chris Walford, described in the report as 'influential' with regards to the Painting team's performance, set up Scott Hardy to score past Building's goalkeeper, Kevin Wakefield and win 2-1.

Sporting Heroes

Seddon has had a long tradition of being involved in sports teams. Football in particular has been a popular choice – although when Ernest Seddon was in charge playing soccer was frowned upon. He feared his workers might get injured and called time on the Seddon team, which played in the 1950s. Unfortunately, no pictures of the side have been traced.

More recently, such restrictions have not been in place and men across the company have played in a variety of leagues and matches – often supporting good causes or playing against customers, suppliers and other contacts.

Another sporting success, this time the Seddon cricket team.
Pictured standing left, Brian Hunter, Clive Russell, Harry Richards, Ray Herbert, Jim Blairs, Maurice Alcock. Bottom left, John Wilburn, Wally Leese, a young Stuart Seddon and Jeff Webb.

Seddon Song

To mark the Seddon centenary in 1997, a musical event was sponsored in Stoke-on-Trent. The celebration was held to mark the creation of the city as a unitary authority.

Newspaper cutting courtesy of The Sentinel.

The Golden Jubilee

In June 2002, Seddon sponsored a giant beacon, at Mow Cop, on the Staffordshire and Cheshire border, to mark The Queen's Golden Jubilee - one of 137 built from Land's End to John O'Groats. The Lord Lieutenant of Staffordshire, James Hawley, lit the beacon, situated next to Mow Cop Castle, to the delight of hundreds of people who assembled to watch the event. Such was the fierce nature of the blaze that the emergency services received calls from worried residents who feared a major fire had broken out.

Newspaper cuttings courtesy of The Sentinel.

IN his message to the City, Group Chairman Mr John Seddon, pictured above, says:

"For many years now Seddon (Stoke) Limited has been supportive of the training and development of young people, and we welcome this opportunity to demonstrate our commitment in the City.

"Throughout its history, Seddon (Stoke) Limited has maintained strong links though construction projects in the city of Stoke-on-Trent and welcome this opportunity to cement future relationships at the start of their Unitary status in the same year as the Seddon Group of companies are celebrating the Centenary of the formation of the Seddon family building business in Lancashire in 1879."

The Sentinel

Beacon shines out to round off Queen's Golden Jubilee celebrations

PURE GOLD

Beautiful Shoes

EIGHT PAGES OF STREET PARTY COLOUR PICTURES BEGIN ON PAGE 19

Jubilee beacon sparks families' alerts

A Community Role

In 2003, Stuart Seddon enjoyed a 12 month term in office as National President of the Painting and Decorating Association, the trade body for painters in the UK. Working with the Association he has played a role in developing a number of policies and initiatives, including working more closely with the industry in Europe.

The menu card for the Association's national banquet, presided over by Stuart Seddon.

PAINTING AND DECORATING ASSOCIATION

Second National Conference Banquet 2003

Stratford Manor Hotel, Stratford-upon-Avon
25th October 2003
National President: Mr Stuart Seddon

Stuart Seddon, in the chains of office as President of the Painting and Decorating Association, with his family.

WINNER

Construction News
QUALITY IN CONSTRUCTION AWARDS 2006

TRAINING ACHIEVEMENT
Seddon (Stoke) Ltd

In March 2006, Seddon (Stoke) won the Quality in Construction Awards' Training Achievement category.

Chapter 8   On a Learning Curve

Apprentices And The Training Ethos

From the earliest days, a commitment to training has been a central part of Seddon (Stoke) Limited's philosophy. The company has operated a dedicated apprentice training scheme since the 1940s, which has been fundamental to the growth and success of the business overall.

Today this scheme spans the entire UK and has produced on average some 40 skilled workers a year through a three-year training programme – in both construction and painting.

As well as training hundreds of young people over the years for trades – plus older people on New Deal labour programmes - the professions are also catered for, with some 30 trainees annually sponsored through university and college in subjects such as Quantity Surveying.

Seddon policy has been – and remains to be – to train from within the company. For decades, talented youngsters with potential have been earmarked and promoted into higher roles within the organisation

That training policy does not only extend to staff, but the Seddon family too. Stuart Seddon is not only a fourth generation member to lead the company – he's also a fourth generation fully-trained bricklayer in the family.

Mike Philo, Seddon (Stoke's) Human Resources manager pictured with apprentices in 2004.

His Great-Grandfather John, his Grandfather Ernest, and his father John all trained as bricklayers – and that was a matter of record in the family. At the company's Annual General Meeting, in April 1952, Ernest Seddon expressed his pleasure that *'his eldest son John is going to start bricklaying for the company in 3 to 4 weeks' time.'*

Stuart's apprenticeship – held under the watchful eye of Ken Podmore and Foreman Roy Grocott, started in 1977 and lasted three years. His first contract was at Henshall Hall in Congleton and he also worked on other projects in Birmingham and Stoke-on-Trent.

Sarah Davis, Eric Braddock and Martin Amison at the Building People Event in 2005, held as part of National Construction Week, where school-leavers went along to Stoneleigh in Warwickshire to see about a career in construction.

Ultimately, good training creates a stable environment for employed staff, generating a feeling of belonging. Many of the young apprentices are supervised on site by former apprentices who completed their training decades ago.

Receiving the Investor In People Standard in 1999.

In 1999, Seddon (Stoke) secured the Investor In People standard for its training policy. Since then training methods have been constantly updated, and more innovative schemes have been introduced. These include bringing on board clients – such as residents in social housing schemes – into apprenticeship programmes and hosting and improving training across the community.

An Early Start

In the 1940s and 1950s, there was a need to accommodate National Service during apprenticeships. Youngsters signed up to serve with Seddon before spending their allotted time in the Armed Forces. Ray Herbert recalls that Ken Sproston – who joined as a trainee and became Transport Manager - would regularly write to Ernest Seddon about his experiences in the military. Ray – who used to spend holidays working at

Seddon while completing his National Service – also remembered that one youngster told Ernest he was learning to drive trucks in the Army. Ernest was pleased to hear it, and told the teenager he could drive the cement mixer when he started back at the company.

Parental involvement was an important aspect of the Apprenticeship appointment. The Deed Of Apprenticeship was a lengthy legal document, signed by construction companies such as Seddon, who were referred to as the 'Master' in the documents. The youngster's parents were referred to as the 'Guardians' and the young persons themselves, known as 'the Apprentices.' Finally, the Deeds were overseen by 'the Representative,' someone selected by the Local Joint Apprenticeship Committee, constituted by the National Joint Council for the Building Industry. All

These pictures taken at Tern Hill Barracks in the late 1940s show some of the young apprentices on-site – dressed in smart overalls. Included in the photograph is Ray Herbert, (fourth from left) who – as described in Chapter Six - went on to become a General Foreman and clocked up 51 years' service with the company.

Safety clothing, such as today's high viz vests and hard hats, were not a part of the 1940s construction scene.

four parties would sign the Deed during a ceremony, which was often an exciting time for the youngster, signalling their coming of age.

Peter Grocott's Deed of Apprenticeship, **(pictured right)** signed in 1952 was a document typical of the time. He signed the Deed at the age of 15, to train as a Joiner, for a trial period of twelve months. Following a successful trial, the contract was extended to five years. In 1957, Peter went on to complete his National Service with the Army, before being re-employed afterwards.

With National Service removed later in the 1950s, apprenticeships became a more straightforward affair. Tony Swindells **(pictured bottom right with Dora Seddon)** signed his Articles, **(pictured below)** in 1955. During the first year, pay was 55 shillings a week, increasing to more than 66 shillings in the second year, 100 shillings in the third year and 125 shillings a week in the fourth. Tony went on to become a qualified Quantity Surveyor.

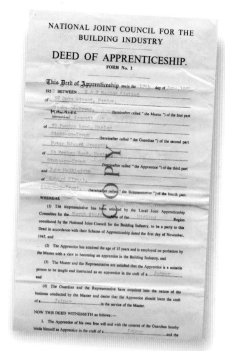

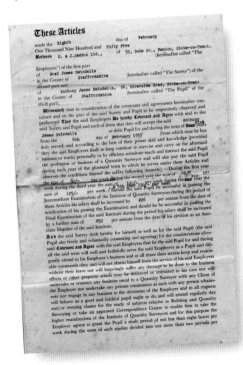

A fresh-faced
Clive Russell.

Neil Hand and Mark Brindley, the joint Managing
Directors of J & S Seddon (Painting) Limited, who
both joined the company after school as trainees.

Home Grown Talent

Clive Russell is typical of the Seddon policy of nurturing
young talent. Starting out as a fresh-faced 15-year-old
working in quantity surveying, he made the jump from
young trainee through to director level – eventually
becoming Managing Director of the Painting company. He
joined initially as a site clerk on £3.50 a week. At his first
interview, Clive had to undertake a test lasting almost two
hours in mental arithmetic and he also had to produce a
technical drawing.

 At his first job, Clive was collected by a Seddon canopied
lorry outside a launderette in Heron Cross, but it went on
to deliver him to the wrong site – flats in Newcastle-under-
Lyme instead of houses in Dalehall, Burslem. However,
once he got to the right place it was a case of straight to
work, under the guidance of site clerk Bill Wilson and
foreman George Allen.

Once talent-spotted himself, in turn Clive went on to
identify managerial skills in Neil Hand and Mark Brindley.
Both started their careers in the industry as teenagers in
the 1980s - Mark as a YTS junior surveyor and Neil as an
apprentice painter. They took over as joint Managing
Directors when Clive retired in 2005.

Jim Blairs.

Whilst studying Quantity
Surveying full-time, Jim
Blairs undertook a period
of work experience in the
1960s on Seddon's Stoke-
on-Trent College
construction site, in
Moorland Road, Burslem.
While there, John Seddon approached him with the offer
of a job. John told Jim that he would put the youngster
through training at night school and day release. Jim
accepted the offer and eventually went on to become
Managing Director of the Building company.

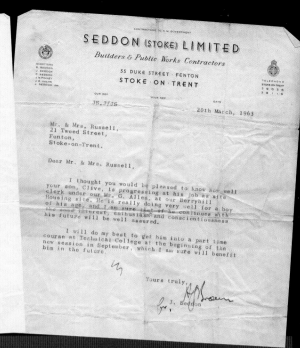

These letters, from John Seddon, were written to Clive Russell and his parents, showing how much joining the company was a family affair. The first outlines the details of Clive's first day with the company in 1962. The second, written in 1963, gives an insight into his performance and the attributes, which were already marking him out for a successful career with the company.

Jim Blairs presents Lee Hartley with commemorative crystal glass to mark success in his studies. Lee achieved a First Class degree in Quantity Surveying on day release in 2006.

Another First Class Degree was achieved by Darren Fowler in the same year as Lee. Darren has trained with the company since leaving school and works as an estimator.

University. Lee completed his training on day-release over an eight-year period.

Training in the Community

As well as training within the company, Seddon has also recognised the value of training in the wider arena.

Ernest Seddon helped play a major part in the training development of the region in his position with the North Staffordshire Apprenticeship Committee. Ernest set this committee up, along with local educationalist, Charles Knapper, and another builder, Bill Leake.

Lee Hartley's **(pictured overleaf)** hard labour reflects what can be achieved with an enthusiastic, committed approach. Lee started in the construction industry labouring on a building site – and went on to achieve a First Class Honours degree in Quantity Surveying, with support from Seddon. Lee joined the company after spotting a job advert for a Trainee Quantity Surveyor after leaving sixth form college – when he was labouring on a building site for some money. He completed an ONC and a HNC before taking his degree at Sheffield's Hallam

This picture shows Roy Baker in the 1980s, at RAF Fairford in Gloucestershire as a teenage painter – he became a foreman at 21. More recently, health and safety has led a shift towards a different style of workwear and checked shirts and jeans of the 1980s have moved on for Seddon painters to be replaced by white aprons, caps and – in certain areas – hi viz vests and hard hats. Roy joined Seddon in the 1980s under a YTS scheme and went on to become Commercial Manager.

Pictured at the Partnering In Action seminar, left to right, Stuart Seddon, Chairman of Seddon (Stoke), Dennis Lenard and Barry Thompson, Director of J & S Seddon (Building) Limited in Stoke-on-Trent.

Seddon's work training and informing within the wider community extended to a Partnering In Action seminar, in 2004, held at Keele University. The event, organised to discuss the future of Partnering contracts in the construction industry, attracted hundreds of construction professionals from across the West Midlands and beyond. Dennis Lenard, the Chief Executive of Constructing Excellence, was the guest speaker.

Dennis Lenard at the Partnering In Action Conference, addressing the audience.

Some of the delegates at the seminar.

Each year, Seddon's Painting company holds an Apprentice of the Year contest, where a youngster training within the company is selected for the title on the basis of their attitude to work, college reports and commitment to learning. The award ceremony is held at Seddon's traditional Christmas party.

Three recent Apprentices of the Year, Tracy Jordan **(left)**, James Johnson **(bottom left)** both working on site, and Martin Amison **(pictured below)** with Stuart Seddon at the 2005 Christmas party receiving his award.

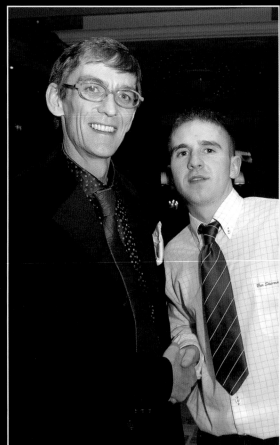

Apprentice of the Year 2006, James Phillips, pictured with Stuart Seddon.

Staff training and commitment to environmental issues - led by Neil Fraser, Seddon's expert in this important area – resulted in the company receiving the environmental standard ISO 14001 in 2004. This picture shows members of the Seddon (Stoke) Board of Directors at that time, including Roger Dean, at the centre of the back row. Roger is a Non-Executive Director. Ian Pinnington, pictured far right, the Company Secretary in 2004, is no longer with the company and the position is now held by Alan Teague.

Representative for more than 25 years. This role also involved settling disputes between apprentices, parents, employers and, sometimes, the College. The forum for all this work was in the North Staffordshire Local Joint Training Committee. When Ernest retired, his son John took on the role, both as Signing Representative and then Chairman.

As the industry got back into its stride after the war Ernest contacted Charles Knapper, an Architect by profession who had just been appointed as the Principal of The College of Building - located in an old pottery on Stoke Road, alongside the Caldon Canal. Together they hatched a plan to get apprentice tradesmen to go to college for technical training. Prior to this, apprentices were bound to their master tradesman by contract and all skills were learnt on site. Any apprentice who wanted technical education found a night school where they attended of their own choice.

John also played his part in the region's educational structure through his association with Stoke-on-Trent College for many years. John originally joined as a member of the Board of Governors in the 1960s, and then a member of the college's Corporation when it became independent from local authority management. Eventually, John became vice chairman of the Corporation. He retired from the post in 2001.

Ernest invited Charles to visit Seddon sites to talk to the boys and their tradesmen during the lunch break. Ernest was a prominent member of the National Federation of Building Trades' Employers and in this capacity he persuaded his colleagues then to allow Charles and himself to visit their sites in a recruitment drive to promote technical training.

A theme of community involvement has continued over the decades. For a number of years, Seddon has played a part in the Safety Health Awareness Day, organised by the Working Well Together Initiative in Staffordshire. Seddon's Director of Support Services, Chris Comerford, has helped organise this annual event, which targets small construction companies of between one and 15 staff and offers them advice that they otherwise would find difficult to access. Seddon has also played a part in the North Staffordshire Health and Safety Group for many years.

The College expanded quickly and the National Apprenticeship Scheme was formed. Boys, their parents, their Employer and the Industry all signed the Deed of Apprenticeship – as shown on page 151.

Ernest held the position of Industry Signing

In the county of Staffordshire, Seddon has been an annual sponsor of the 'Bridging the Gap' competition. Run in conjunction with the CITB Construction Skills, Staffordshire Partnership and Staffordshire County Council, this initiative aims to encourage interest in a construction career among youngsters.

The delegates at the Seddon Health and Safety Day 2005 watch a safety video.

At the Britannia Stadium, home of Stoke City FC, Seddon introduced its own Health and Safety Day in 2005. The event attracted people from across the UK, both Seddon staff and subcontractors. One of the guests was Ian Whittingham MBE who has been an active campaigner for improved health and safety in the construction industry since a fall from a roof on a building site left him confined to a wheelchair.

Centre of Excellence

In 2002, Seddon opened a dedicated training centre, on Fenton Industrial Estate. Stoke-on-Trent Lord Mayor, Ellis Bevan officially cut the ribbon at the two-storey centre, which included a classroom environment and working area in purpose-built surroundings, where trainees could study without distractions.

The Seddon Training Centre opened in 2002 on the Fenton Industrial Estate.

Proud Times

Seddon enjoyed proud times in 2005 and 2006, when their work in training gained national recognition.

In November 2005, Stoke-on-Trent College announced that their new multi-million pound training centre – where trades including bricklaying, painting and decorating and plumbing are taught – was to be named The John Seddon Building Technology Centre in honour of John Seddon's contribution to education in the Stoke area. Funded by the regional development agency Advantage West Midlands, the Learning and Skills Council and Stoke-on-Trent College, the high-technology facility bears no comparison to the facilities John Seddon himself studied in at the college in 1952, which were then based in a converted bottle kiln.

Hundreds of people attended the opening event – including some of Seddon's own apprentices who studied at the college, the elected mayor of Stoke-on-Trent Mark Meredith, Graham Moore OBE, Principal of Stoke-on-Trent College, Kevin Farrell, the Chairman of the College's Corporation, and John Edwards, Chief Executive of Advantage West Midlands.

Modestly, when John Seddon gave a speech at the opening of the centre he said to the crowd: *"Firstly, let me say that it was not my idea that this magnificent new Building Technology Centre should be named after me. In fact, I was persuaded only after much objection – I still think that to name the building after The Seddon Group rather than me would be better – but there you are, I was over-ruled."* John only told his family and colleagues at Seddon days before that the ceremony was due to take place.

Kevin Farrell, Chairman of the College's Corporation, with John Seddon, John Edwards, Chief Executive of Advantage West Midlands and Graham Moore OBE, Principal of Stoke-on-Trent College.

John Seddon cutting the ribbon to the new centre.

The Official Opening of
The John Seddon
Building Technology Centre
at Stoke on Trent College, Burslem Campus
Tuesday 8th November 2005

10.30am	Tours of the Centre followed by Tea and Coffee
11.30am	Welcome and introductions Kevin Farrell, Chairman of Corporation
11.45am	AWM Strategy for Economic Prosperity John Edwards, Chief Executive, Advantage West Midlands
11.55am	Official Opening John Seddon, Seddon Group Limited
12.05pm	Buffet

STOKE on TRENT COLLEGE

CENTRE OF VOCATIONAL EXCELLENCE CONSTRUCTION

A programme for the opening of the John Seddon Building Technology Centre.

John Seddon and his wife Claire are joined by Seddon staff outside the new building.

Later that year, Seddon (Stoke) entered for the *Construction News* Quality in Construction Awards, in the Training Achievement category. This was the first time the company had entered an award of this nature and they were shortlisted from more than 10 entries – including some of the biggest names in the UK construction industry – to the final three.

In March 2006, company representatives made their way to London for the Award's ceremony – held at the Park Lane Hilton in London. The result was kept a strict secret until the event and, as Seddon was announced the winner, **(pictured below)** Jim Blairs, Mike Philo and Garth Nethercot went on stage in front of thousands in the industry to collect the award.

The judges gave the award to the company for what they described as *'it's all embracing approach which, while* admirably serving its own commercial needs, also benefits the wider community.' One judge added: 'For me this was a great example of ethical trading in the local community.'

Just weeks later, Seddon continued their winning streak to take another title, this time on the company's home turf of Stoke-on-Trent, where they secured the Investor In People accolade – sponsored by the Learning and Skills Council - at The Sentinel Business Awards, held at the Moat House Hotel. Chris Comerford, Director of Support Services went on stage to receive the award.

The same award was secured by 4m flooring uk, part of Seddon (Stoke), who entered the contest in 2004. Mark Holden, 4m's Managing Director, received the accolade.

Both pictures courtesy of The Sentinel

The team at 4m flooring uk, pictured in 2002 when the company became part of Seddon (Stoke) Ltd.

Chapter 9

A National Reach

The Role Of Seddon (Stoke) Across The UK

Fifty years after setting up as an official company within The Potteries, Seddon (Stoke) has gone on to become a national organisation in its own right.

With offices across England, Wales and Scotland, it has established a presence across Britain and offers the service and support of a national contractor.

Much of the expansion has been within the last ten years, with Partnering contracts in particular offering the stability and opportunity to gain a wider geographical spread.

In 2007, the Painting company had 26 offices across England, Scotland and Wales. The Building company had 6 offices, stretching across the West and East Midlands, into the South West and both North and South Wales.

At all regional offices, people local to the area are employed and the centres play their part in the social and economic make-up of their particular region, with a number of good causes supported and initiatives implemented at a local level to support the area.

The working patterns of 4m flooring uk enable the company to retain its one office, based in Crewe, although it works across England, Scotland, Wales, Ireland and even into parts of Europe.

This picture shows that in 1982, the Silver Jubilee year of Seddon (Stoke), the company had Painting offices in Burslem, Middlesbrough, York and Newcastle-upon-Tyne and there were three Building offices at Birmingham, Chester and Congleton – all supported by the headquarters of Seddon (Stoke) in Fenton.

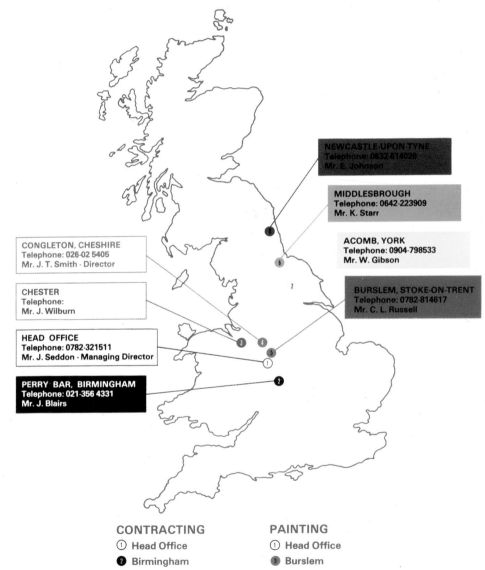

SEDDON (STOKE) LIMITED

NEWCASTLE-UPON-TYNE
Telephone: 0632-614026
Mr. E. Johnson

MIDDLESBROUGH
Telephone: 0642-223909
Mr. K. Starr

CONGLETON, CHESHIRE
Telephone: 026-02 5405
Mr. J. T. Smith - Director

ACOMB, YORK
Telephone: 0904-798533
Mr. W. Gibson

CHESTER
Telephone:
Mr. J. Wilburn

BURSLEM, STOKE-ON-TRENT
Telephone: 0782-814617
Mr. C. L. Russell

HEAD OFFICE
Telephone: 0782-321511
Mr. J. Seddon - Managing Director

PERRY BAR, BIRMINGHAM
Telephone: 021-356 4331
Mr. J. Blairs

CONTRACTING
1. Head Office
2. Birmingham
3. Chester
4. Congleton

PAINTING
1. Head Office
5. Burslem
6. Middlesbrough
7. York
8. Newcastle-upon-Tyne

Regional Offices

Birmingham
Tel No: 0121 331 4329
Fax No: 0121 356 4331
birmingham@seddonbuilding.co.uk

Birmingham (Maintenance)
Tel No: 0121 344 3899
Fax No: 0121 344 4843
sms@seddonbuilding.co.uk

Derby
Tel No: 01332 348543
Fax No: 01332 345426
eastmidlands@seddonbuilding.co.uk

North Wales & Cheshire
Tel No: 01244 520705
Fax No: 01244 537652
chester@seddonbuilding.co.uk

Merthyr Tydfil
Tel No: 01443 692077
Fax No: 01443 692256
merthyr@seddonbuilding.co.uk

Normanton
Tel No: 01924 898148
Fax No: 01924 895703
normanton@seddonbuilding.co.uk

Stafford
Tel No: 01785 256300
Fax No: 01785 270771
stafford@seddonbuilding.co.uk

Stoke-on-Trent
Tel No: 01782 599511
Fax No: 01782 599682
enquiries@seddonbuilding.co.uk

Wotton-under-Edge
Tel No: 01453 842391
Fax No: 01453 521255
enquiries@jotchamkendall.co.uk

This map of Building Offices, shows the company's presence in 2007.

Another map identifying Painting Offices across Britain in 2007.

Regional Offices

Airdrie
Tel No: 01236 761156
Fax No: 01236 779125
airdrie@seddonpainting.co.uk

Andover
Tel No: 01264 336773
Fax No: 01264 364211
andover@seddonpainting.co.uk

Birmingham
Tel No: 0121 359 3954
Fax No: 0121 359 5880
birmingham@seddonpainting.co.uk

Borough Green
Tel No: 01732 883444
Fax No: 01732 887159
southeast@seddonpainting.co.uk

Boston
Tel No: 01205 358392
Fax No: 01205 359951
boston@seddonpainting.co.uk

Bristol
Tel No: 01179 381 001
Fax No: 01179 380 200
bristol@seddonpainting.co.uk

Burton on Trent
Tel No: 01283 539601
Fax No: 01283 539601
burton@seddonpainting.co.uk

Cheltenham
Tel No: 01242 222035
Fax No: 01242 262109
cheltenham@seddonpainting.co.uk

Exeter
Tel No: 01179 381 001
Fax No: 01179 380 200
exeter@seddonpainting.co.uk

Gateshead
Tel No: 0191 491 3060
Fax No: 0191 491 1740
gateshead@seddonpainting.co.uk

Huntingdon
Tel No: 01480 426540
Fax No: 01480 426541
eastanglia@seddonpainting.co.uk

Leicester
Tel No: 0116 277 8666
Fax No: 0116 277 4267
leicester@seddonpainting.co.uk

Nottingham
Tel No: 0115 977 1357
Fax No: 0115 976 4020
nottingham@seddonpainting.co.uk

Merthyr Tydfil
Tel No: 01443 692077
Fax No: 01443 692256
merthyr@seddonpainting.co.uk

Preston
Tel No: 01772 201771
Fax No: 01772 201772
preston@seddonpainting.co.uk

Scunthorpe
Tel No: 01724 282468
Fax No: 01724 282469
scunthorpe@seddonpainting.co.uk

St Clears
Tel No: 01994 230077
Fax No: 01994 230077
westwales@seddonpainting.co.uk

Stoke-on-Trent
Tel No: 01782 598000
Fax No: 01782 598101
stoke@seddonpainting.co.uk

Southampton
Tel No: 023 804 57684
Fax No: 023 804 57685
southampton@seddonpainting.co.uk

Telford
Tel No: 01952 588228
Fax No: 01952 587160
telford@seddonpainting.co.uk

Watford
Tel No: 01923 256113
Fax No: 01923 256162
watford@seddonpainting.co.uk

Wigton
Tel No: 01697 371978
Fax No: 01697 371978
cumbria@seddonpainting.co.uk

Wrexham
Tel No: 01978 660408
Fax No: 01978 660485
wrexham@seddonpainting.co.uk

York
Tel No: 01904 798533
Fax No: 01904 782331
york@seddonpainting.co.uk

A Snapshot Of Seddon In The UK

Building Offices

DERBY

Opened in the early 1990s, the Derby office was opened on the strength of a large contract with British Telecom in the area. The office was originally based in Shardlow, just south of the city, but later moved to the prestigious new industrial development at Pride Park.

Mick Bull **(pictured left)** of Seddon in Derby at a church building project with Father Murphy of St. Alban's Church in the city.

NORMANTON

Seddon (Building) has had a presence in Yorkshire for some 20 years, initially with an office in Harrogate. The Harrogate office was mainly involved in maintenance contracts and refurbishment. However, in 2002, the Harrogate Office closed and the office in Normanton opened, with more emphasis on general building contracts.

BIRMINGHAM

In 2006, the Birmingham team (pictured right) moved into new premises in Summer Lane, Newtown. The office has undertaken major projects across the area, including a high profile new arts centre in Bromsgrove and high technology facilities at a school in Bewdley.

Birmingham is also home to Seddon's new Maintenance company (pictured left). This was formed in 2007, after Birmingham pioneered a new venture, Seddon Maintenance Services, for the West Midlands region several years ago. The new Maintenance company has been rolled out across the UK and is a joint venture between the Building and Painting companies.

STOKE-ON-TRENT

In 2006, J & S Seddon (Building) moved its Stoke-on-Trent regional office into new facilities at Duke Street in Fenton. The office now has its own centre, having previously shared a building with Head Office. The Stoke regional office has undertaken a clutch of major deals, including the multi-million pound Bentilee Neighbourhood Centre, the Bevan Lee regeneration project in Cannock and a housing development for older people in Meir for Staffordshire Housing Association.

NORTH WALES

Situated in Flintshire, the North Wales office is the main operating base for contracts in North Wales and Cheshire. It employs 60 staff, half of whom are Welsh speaking, and is proud to be a company with a strong regional identity. The office works mainly in the public sector on new build, refurbishment and maintenance contracts and was opened in the mid 1970s.

STAFFORD

The Stafford office was formed as part of a the major partnering contract with Staffordshire County Council in 2003. It has created job opportunities and economic growth in the area. Works with Staffordshire County Council range from small works to large refurbishment projects and the local authority is one of Seddon's oldest customers.

JOTCHAM AND KENDALL

Based at Wotton-under-Edge in Gloucestershire, Jotcham & Kendall Ltd was bought by J & S Seddon (Building) in 1999.

The company has an historic past. It was started in 1680 by John and Richard Jotcham with the conversion of the Church House of St James' Church in Charfield.

The Jotcham and Kendall office also works closely with the Building company's satellite office based in Merthyr Tydfil, South Wales.

Painting Offices

AIRDRIE

Opened in the late 1990s, the Airdrie office of J & S Seddon (Painting) has undertaken major works across the length and breadth of Scotland.

Over the years, representatives from the office have set in place a company tradition, wearing kilts and traditional Scottish dress for the company's annual Christmas party.

BIRMINGHAM

J & S Seddon (Painting) opened an office in Birmingham in 1996. Ten years later the company had continued to grow and moved into new premises in Perry Barr in 2006.

BOROUGH GREEN AND WATFORD

The move south by J & S Seddon (Painting) has been a rewarding one for the company. The Borough Green office was opened around the same time as Watford, to give the company a strategic presence north and south of London. The offices have gone from strength to strength since opening in 2004 and secured the largest painting contract the company had ever won with a £10 million deal with London & Quadrant in 2005. In 2007, London & Quadrant named the company their Contractor of the Year at their prestigious Maintenance awards.

BRISTOL

J & S Seddon (Painting) first opened an office in Bristol in 1996 and moved to new premises in 2002. The office continues to go from strength to strength, in particular working across the social housing sector and within military environments. Its work is supported in the South West by the regional office at Exeter, which opened in 2005.

BURTON-ON-TRENT

The Burton-on-Trent office was opened in 2003 on the strength of two main contracts in the area, with Trent and Dove Housing Association and Homezone Housing Association. This picture shows representatives from the company signing a partnership deal with Trent and Dove Housing Association.

CHELTENHAM

One of the earliest painting regional offices, Cheltenham has been another success story for Seddon since it opened in 1988. The office has carried out work for a wide range of clients, working within social housing, education, local authority and military environments, as well as the commercial and industrial sector.

LEICESTER

Leicester office has pioneered new and innovative ways of working closely with the community to deliver the best working practices. Recruiting local tenants as apprentices and events aimed at encouraging young people to train as painters have been some of its initiatives.

EAST ANGLIA

Opened in 2005, the East Anglia office was originally a satellite of the Leicester Office. It is based in Huntingdon.

MERTHYR TYDFIL AND ST CLEARS

Merthyr Tydfil office opened in 1996 and in 2004 the company's presence in South Wales was stepped up with the opening of another office in St Clears. Both offices have been successful in working with local authorities and the social housing sector.

NOTTINGHAM

The Nottingham office is shared with Seddons (Plant and Engineers) a company which is part of Seddon Group. It opened in 1990 and is supported in the East Midlands by the Boston and Scunthorpe offices.

PRESTON

Preston-based painting company, Dennis Kehoe, was bought by J & S Seddon (Painting) in 2003.

The company was bought as a venture into the ecclesiastical and heritage market, which was Dennis Kehoe's main area of work. The Preston office still works mainly in this sector, but with additional work in social housing, health and education.

SOUTHAMPTON

Southampton University, the National Oceanography Centre, Places for People and the Ministry of Defence – at Salisbury Plain and Blandford in Dorset – are just some of J & S Seddon (Painting's) clients in and around the city.

STOKE-ON-TRENT
The Stoke regional office of J & S Seddon (Painting) is located in Oldfield House, the new state-of-the-art centre for the company, which was opened in 2006.

YORK
The York office is the oldest regional centre for J & S Seddon (Painting), opened in 1962. It remains in its original office, based in Acomb. It has worked for many years at military sites across the North of England.

WREXHAM

Wrexham is another long-standing regional office, which opened in the mid-1970s. It moved to new premises in 2003.

GATESHEAD

Places for People, Accent North East Housing Association, Gateshead NHS Trust and Hanover Housing are just some of Gateshead's clients. It works closely with the neighbouring Carlisle office.

Seddon The Story So Far

A celebration of 50 years of Seddon (Stoke) Ltd.

TIMELINE

Timeline – Seddon (Stoke) Ltd

1957   Formation of Seddon (Stoke) Ltd, with Ernest Seddon appointed Chairman of the Board and Jonas Seddon appointed Company Secretary
Jack Finney appointed a Director of Seddon (Stoke)

1958   Jonas Seddon resigned as Company Secretary and Andrew Brown appointed to the position

1959   Mr Jack Hulme appointed Director

1960   John Seddon appointed Director

1961   Purchase of 51 and 53 Duke Street, Fenton completed, later to become part of Seddon (Stoke's) new head office

1962   Building and land purchased at RAF Valley on Anglesey for offices
2, New Lane, Acomb, York purchased as a small yard and office quarters for the Painting Department

1963   Cyril Adams joined the Board
Herbert Blood became Manager of the York Branch
Purchase of 43 – 49 Duke Street, Fenton

3/11/1967   The 21st Christmas Party – ladies given a small present. Gifts of tea sets and glass tankards

1968   Although never officially appointed Managing Director, Ernest Seddon, Company Chairman, had been assumed to be so.
John Seddon formally appointed Managing Director

1969   Jack Hulme retires, but continued to act as a consultant

1970   Peter Mottram to act as Manager of the Painting Department

1971	Decision to close the Anglesey Office due to end of term contracts, Mr Bill Saunders to move back to Stoke area eventually
	Land to be bought at West Street, Congleton for an office for Terry Smith and his staff.
1973	Terry Smith appointed Director
	Jonas Seddon resigned as Director on his 65th birthday
	Gold watches given to 58 employees who had been with the company for 21 years or more
1974	Ernest Seddon relinquished his position as Chairman
	John Seddon elected Chairman
1975	Peter Mottram to be made a Director after running the Painting Department fo several years.
	Jack Hulme died
	Gold watches to be handed to 21 long-serving employees at the annual party
1976	1, Abercorn Street, Fenton, purchased for Painting Department
1977	Agreed rental of land at Old Tramway, Fenton
1978	Apprenticeship for Stuart Seddon
1979	Ken Sproston died
	An offer to purchase property at Westgate Road, Newcastle-upon-Tyne for improved storage facilities is made
	Jack Finney retired
1980	Mr Brian Mellor appointed Company Secretary
	Premises in Perry Barr to be used as a central office for Jim Blairs
1981	Use of new timber framed housing on site was going well. The Chairman reported that this type of housing had a long future.
	Mr Ernest Seddon resigned Directorship. Mr John Seddon paid tribute to the work Ernest had done for Seddon (Stoke) Ltd since its inception in 1957, initially as MD, then as Director. He had worked for Seddon Group for almost 60 years.

1982 Silver Jubilee ash trays were made for clients to commemorate 25 years for Seddon (Stoke) Ltd as a limited company
Painters vacated offices on Duke Street and moved to Abercorn Street, Fenton

1983 Perry Barr Office and depot nearly complete and Jim Blairs and staff moved in
Dave Povey and staff to move into new Chester depot and offices
Frank Seddon to resign directorship

1984 George Allen to retire after 36 years with the company

1985 Frank Seddon died

1987 Ernest Seddon died
Seddon (Stoke) Ltd to undergo reorganisation
More space needed at the Chester Office – to be accommodated within the existing premises at Hawarden
Mr A J Hand retired
Jim Blairs, Bill Gibson, Dave Povey and Clive Russell offered Divisional Directorships
Jack Finney died
Cheltenham Office purchased

1988 Offer made for 270, Duke Street
New fax machine installed
Joe Witkowski, Bill Saunders and Frank Duffy retired
First Equal Opportunity policy issued
Increasing demand from potential clients for a Quality Assurance policy

1989 Seddon (Painting) move into Oldfield Business Park after the summer holiday
Proposed, seconded and resolved that Seddon (Stoke) Ltd to set up 3 new subsidiary companies to acquire and manage the business of building, painting and development:
J & S Seddon (Building) Ltd
J & S Seddon (Painting) Ltd
Viceroy Developments Ltd

1989 *Cont.*   Middlesbrough Office closed
Mr Ken Starr to take early retirement
Painting move from Hot Lane to Oldfield Business Park

1991   Gary Owen named Painting Apprentice of the Year
Painting's marketing literature updated to include office relocations at
Southampton, Carlisle and Wrexham
Asked for volunteers for early retirement and redundancy to reduce the
management and staff levels
Chairman comments that "...*he had never in his 30 years' experience known
conditions as bad as at present.*"
Stuart Seddon expressed some concern over the Hard Hat, COSHH & Noise
Regulations
Dave Povey to take early retirement

1992   Insurance premiums hit due to problems of stolen company cars – gear locks
and fuel cut-offs considered
John Seddon urges Stuart Seddon and Clive Russell to try out the new diesel
cars.

1993   Vaughan Cartwright appointed Divisional Director in May
Steve Owen offered a position as Divisional Director based at Birmingham
40 mobile phones were costing £70,000 a year and pagers £7,000 – not
including the cost of purchase
All outlying offices had been issued with PCs and printers

1994   Peter Mottram resigns as Chairman of Painting and Clive Russell and Stuart
Seddon made joint Managing Directors
Vaughan Cartwright appointed Director
John Seddon intended to stay as Chairman, but released the position of MD
to Stuart Seddon.
Complaints regarding passive smoking in vans and the office – if co-
operation could not be achieved, then a no smoking policy would have to be
considered
John Seddon asked to join the Board of The Britannia Building Society as
Non-Executive Director. This would reduce the amount of time he would
spend at Seddon (Stoke) and he would hand over more duties to Stuart and
Brian Mellor
Proposal to invite John Wilburn to become Divisional Director with
responsibility for the Chester Office

1994 Cont.   Barry Thompson to become Divisional Director with a specific role as Chief Estimator
Quality Standard ISO 9001 achieved

1995   Employees working for Viceroy Developments had been taken under the wing of the Building Company
Barry Thompson appointed Director
Jim Blairs and Stuart Seddon appointed joint Managing Directors of the Building company and John Seddon became Non-Executive Chairman
Centenary logo and celebrations to be organised for the following year
Latham Bill receives Royal Ascent

1997   Seddon Group 100 years old
Russell White, Alan Liddell and Geoff Williams become Divisional Directors
Harry Richards appointed Divisional Director for the Stoke-on-Trent area
The My City Project had been set up as a joint venture between Seddon and Stoke-on-Trent City Council during 1997, at a cost of £10,000 to Seddon. There would be a 12 month calendar of events, first of which to be held at the Northwood Stadium

1998   John Seddon resigned as Chairman – Stuart Seddon to take over
Shortage of labour – difficulties in recruiting across the whole company

1999   Mark Brindley made Divisional Director
Steve Owen made Divisional Director for Birmingham operations
Kevin Wood made Divisional Director for East Midlands and Harrogate
Jotcham & Kendall purchased
Brian Mellor resigned as Company Secretary - Ian Pinnington appointed Company Secretary
Neil Hand appointed Divisional Director
Company achieves Investor In People Standard

2000   Alan Nixon to be promoted to Chief Estimator
Steve Owen appointed Director

2001   Chris Comerford appointed Divisional Director for Support Services of Seddon (Stoke) Ltd
John Wilburn to retire after 30 years with the company

2002	Proposed move of East Midlands Office from Shardlow to Pride Park, Derby
	Seddon Business Solutions set up
	Purchase of 4m flooring uk
2003	Peter Hordley and Alan Nixon appointed Divisional Directors
	ISO14001 achieved
2004	John Seddon did not wish to be re-elected to the Board, but would remain
	Non-Executive Director of Seddon (Stoke) Ltd
	Alan Nixon elected Director
	Partnering Action Seminar at Keele very successful
2005	Clive Russell retires as Managing Director of the Painting company
	Mark Brindley and Neil Hand become joint Managing Directors
	Forty extra staff taken on at Borough Green due to the London & Quadrant contract
	J & S Seddon (Painting) report an increase in profit of more than 33% on the previous best year of 2003
	More offices acquired in Cambridge and Exeter
	Geoff Major appointed Divisional Director
	Seddon (Stoke) to sponsor the Waddington Suite at Stoke City F.C.
2006	Chris Pritchard made Regional Director
	Jim Blairs retiring as Managing Director of Building with effect from end of 2006, after more than 41 years' service
	Alan Nixon to take on the role of Managing Director of Building with effect from the November management meeting
2007	Party held to mark the 50th anniversary celebration of Seddon (Stoke) Limited at the International Convention Centre in Birmingham

Author's Note – The Story So Far

Dipping into the lives of Seddon family members and the workers who have built this company up over more than 100 years has been a privilege.

Ultimately, this book is a tribute to all who have played a part in the success of Seddon (Stoke) Ltd. My concern is that people who worked for the company for many years are not mentioned. However, with so many workers completing long service with the company, and so many projects undertaken, including everything in these pages would be an impossible task.

Many people have played a part in this publication and their generous support is indicative of the respect held for Seddon, not just in Stoke-on-Trent, but across the UK. A full list of names appears in the acknowledgements section, but Ian Shaw at The Potteries Museum and Art Gallery, along with representatives from The Sentinel, have played a particularly helpful part in the project.

Sadly one contributor, George Allen **(pictured left)**, who worked for many years at Seddon as a Contracts Manager, died before this book was published.

George Allen

Clive Russell has project managed the book and his energy, drive and enthusiasm has been the major force in delivering it from an initial idea, on to the printing press. Stuart Seddon has been a source of help and guidance and his father John has spent many hours patiently answering many questions and providing a wealth of historical information.

We were delighted to find another fourth generation family business to design and print the book in Stoke-on-Trent. J. H. Brookes (Printers) Ltd., based in Hanley, have treated the entire project with care, patience and the very highest levels of professionalism.

their degree of affection, admiration and respect for the company is reflected within the book.

To sum up, one long-serving Seddon worker described himself and his workfriends as *'Seddon men, through and through, just like rock, cut us through the middle and we've Seddon written throughout.'* I hope this book goes someway to explaining how and why one company has played such an important part in so many people's lives.

Retirees and long-serving employees have willingly given their time to sit together and talk about the past. Recording their stories has been enjoyable, and I hope

Jane Shepherd
March 2007

Some of the Seddon staff, retired and current who provided the information necessary for the production of this book, Eric Braddock, Vince Lockett and George Grocott

More contributions from Seddon's Directors and employees including **(left to right)** Sheila Dobson, Dave Hulson, Harry Richards, Clive Russell and Cyril Wakefield.

(left to right) Arthur Sadler, Clive Russell, George Grocott, John Seddon, John Bentley and Peter Mottram.

Designer Steve Plumb and Studio Manager Phil Green working on the book.

A fourth generation Stoke-on-Trent family business who designed and printed the book in the city, Steve Plumb, Simon Brookes and Phil Green outside Brookes offices in Hanley.

Seddon The Story So Far

A celebration of 50 years of Seddon (Stoke) Ltd.

ACKNOWLEDGEMENTS